Happy Birthday

1000 ACTION WORDS DICTIONARY

ELT EDUCATION (THAILAND) CO.,LTD.
บริษัท อีแอลที เอ็ดยูเคชั่น (ไทยแลนด์) จำกัด

1000 ACTION WORDS DICTIONARY

ผู้แต่ง Dr. Obrom Sinpibarn

ISBN 974-9960-02-5

จัดพิมพ์โดย

บริษัท อีแอลที เอ็ดยูเคชั่น (ไทยแลนด์) จำกัด
15/234 ซอยเสือใหญ่อุทิศ ถ.รัชดาภิเษก แขวงจันทรเกษม
เขตจตุจักร กทม. 10900
15/234 Soi Sua Yai Uthit, Ratchada Phisek Road, Chankasem,
Chatuchak, Bangkok 10900
Tel: 0-2541 7375, 0-2930 6215 Fax: 0-2541 7377, 0-2930 7733
Email: tkeeree@inet.co.th
จัดจำหน่ายโดย
บริษัท ดวงกมลสมัย จำกัด
15/234 ซอยเสือใหญ่อุทิศ ถ.รัชดาภิเษก แขวงจันทรเกษม
เขตจตุจักร กทม. 10900
15/234 Soi Sua Yai Uthit, Ratchada Phisek Road, Chankasem,
Chatuchak, Bangkok 10900
Tel: 0-2541 7375, 0-2930 6215 Fax: 0-2541 7377, 0-2930 7733
Email: dktoday@inet.co.th Website: www.dktoday.net

1000 ACTION WORDS DICTIONARY

Dr. Obrom Sinpibarn

คำนำ

    พจนานุกรมที่มีอยู่ในตลาดขณะนี้มีมากมาย   แต่พจนานุกรมที่เจาะลึกเฉพาะ Action Words ยังไม่มี ซึ่งคำเหล่านี้ล้วนเป็นคำสำคัญอย่างยิ่งในภาษาอังกฤษ ถ้าขาดคำเหล่านี้ไปประโยคจะไม่สมบูรณ์ รูปของ verb เป็นส่วนสำคัญของคำศัพท์ โดยจะช่วยให้ผู้เรียนได้พูดเกี่ยวกับสิ่งที่มนุษย์ได้สร้างขึ้นและสิ่งที่อยู่รอบ ๆ ตัวเรา

    พจนานุกรม 1000 Action Words Dictionary เล่มนี้ทำขึ้นเพื่อแนะนำ verb ที่ใช้กันบ่อย ๆ โดยเฉพาะ รวมทั้ง sigle-word verbs เช่น :- call และ phrasal verbs เช่น call off เป็นต้น

    พจนานุกรมเล่มนี้มีจุดมุ่งหมายสำคัญ 3 ประการ :-

    1. เพื่อเพิ่มศัพท์ใหม่ให้กับผู้เรียน

    2. เพื่อแสดงให้เห็นความแตกต่างระหว่าง verbs ที่มีความหมายคล้ายคลึงกัน เช่น : see, look, glare, stare etc.

3. เพื่อแนะนำความหมายในการใช้ phrasal verbs ที่มีประโยชน์ให้กับผู้เรียน เช่น :- get away, get off, get on และ get up เป็นต้น

สิ่งที่สำคัญอีกอย่างหนึ่งคือนำเอา Action Words ทุกคำมาสร้างเป็นประโยคง่าย ๆ เกี่ยวกับชีวิตประจำวัน พร้อมด้วยคำอ่านและคำแปลอีกด้วย

หวังอย่างยิ่งว่าพจนานุกรมเล่มนี้คงมีประโยชน์ สำหรับผู้ใช้เป็นอย่างยิ่ง

ดร.อบรม สินภิบาล

สารบัญ

A

accept *(แอคเซพท′)* accepting, accepted

Jane accepts a gift from her father.

เจนรับของขวัญจากพ่อของเธอ

ache *(เอค)* aching, ached

Willy's stomach aches because he ate too much.

วิลลีปวดท้องเพราะเขากินมากเกินไป

act *(แอ็คท)* acting, acted

Jimmy acted as a wolf in the school play.

จิมมีแสดงเป็นสุนัขป่าในละครโรงเรียน

add *(แอ็ด)* adding, added

Mother is adding some milk

to the coffee.

แม่เพิ่มนมในกาแฟ

add up *(แอ็ด อั้พ)*

Teacher asked me to add up these numbers.

ครูขอร้องให้ผมบวกตัวเลขเหล่านี้

admire *(แอ็ดไมร์)* admiring, admired

Jane's friends admire her beautiful new doll.

เพื่อนของเจนชื่นชมตุ๊กตาสวยงาม
ตัวใหม่ของเธอ

advise *(แอ็ดไฝส์)* advising, advised

The policeman advised us to cross the road carefully.

ตำรวจแนะนำให้เราข้ามถนนอย่าง
ระมัดระวัง

agree *(อักรี่)* agreeing, agreed

Peter agreed to help me with

my bags.

ปีเตอร์ยินดีที่จะช่วยหิ้วกระเป๋าให้ฉัน

aim *(เอม´)* aiming, aimed

Andy aims carefully at the apple.

แอนดีเล็งไปที่แอปเปิ้ลด้วยความระ-
มัดระวัง

allow *(แอ็ลเลา´)* allowing, allowed

Dogs are not allowed in the station.

ไม่อนุญาตให้นำสุนัขเข้ามาในสถานี
รถไฟ

amuse *(อัมยูส´)* amusing, amused

The crown amused us with his tricks.

ตัวตลกทำให้เราขบขันด้วยลูกเล่น
ของเขา

answer *(อ่านเซอะ)* answering, answered

Helen is answering the telephone.

เฮเลนกำลังพูดโทรศัพท์อยู่

appear *(แอ็พเพีย′)* appearing, appeared

A bright star appeared suddenly in the sky.

ดาวที่สุกสกาวปรากฏขึ้นทันทีทันใดบนท้องฟ้า

arrange *(แอะเร′นจ)* arranging, arranged

Father is arranging the bags on the shelf.

พ่อกำลังจัดกระเป๋าบนหิ้ง

ask *(อาซค)* asking, asked

I asked mother for another slice of cake.

ผมขอขนมเค้กจากแม่อีกหนึ่งชิ้น

attack *(แอ็ทแทค̍)* attacking, attacked

> The fierce dog attacked the burglar.
>
> สุนัขที่ดุทำร้ายนักย่องเบา

attend *(แอ็ทเทน̍ด)* attending, attended

> We are attending Jane's birthday party.
>
> เรากำลังอยู่ในงานเลี้ยงวันเกิดของเจน

awake *(อะเวค̍)* awaking, awoke

> The alarm clock awoke me from sleep.
>
> นาฬิกาปลุกปลุกฉันให้ตื่น

B

bake *(เบค)* baking, baked

> Mother is baking a cake for

Kathy's birthday.

แม่กำลังอบเค้กสำหรับวันเกิดของ
แคธี

balance *(แบ′ลแอ็นซ)* balancing, balanced

Andy is balancing a ball on
his forehead.

แอนดีกำลังเลี้ยงลูกบอลบนหน้า
ผากของเขา

bandage *(แบ′นดิจ)* bandaging, bandaged

The nurse is bandaging Jim's
arm.

พยาบาลกำลังพันแผลที่แขนของ
จิมมี

barbecue *(บ′าบิคยู)* barbecuing, barbecued

Father is barbecuing in the
backyard.

พ่อกำลังย่างเนื้ออยู่ที่สนามหลังบ้าน

bark *(บาค)* barking, barked

> The dogs are barking loudly at the cat.
>
> สุนัขกำลังเห่าแมวเสียงดัง

bath *(บั้ธ)* bathing, bathed

> Mother baths the baby in warm water.
>
> แม่อาบน้ำให้ลูกน้อยในน้ำอุ่น

beat *(บีท)* beating, beat

> Mother is beating an egg.
>
> แม่กำลังตีไข่

beg *(เบ็ก)* begging, begged

> The clever dog begs for a bone.
>
> สุนัขแสนรู้ขอกระดูก

belong *(บิล′อง)* belonging, belonged

> This book belongs to me. It is mine.

หนังสือเป็นของผม มันเป็นของผม

bend *(เบ็นด)* bending, bent

Willy is bending a stick.

วิลลีกำลังหักไม้

bite *(ไบท)* biting, bit

The dog is biting a bone.

สุนัขกำลังแทะกระดูก

bleed *(บลีด)* bleeding, bled

Jimmy's arm is bleeding.

เลือดกำลังไหลออกจากแขนของ
จิมมี

block *(บล็อก)* blocking, blocked

The fallen tree is blocking the
road.

ต้นไม้ที่ล้มกีดขวางถนนอยู่

blow *(บโล)* blowing, blew

The wind is blowing through
the trees.

ลมกำลังพัดผ่านต้นไม้

blow out *(บโล เอ๊าท)*

Jane blows out the candles on her birthday cake.

เจนเป่าเทียนบนเค้กวันเกิดของเธอ

blow up *(บโล อั๊พ)*

Andy is blowing up a balloon.

แอนดีกำลังเป่าลูกโป่งอยู่

blush *(บลัฌ)* blushing, blushed

Linda blushed when Jimmy gave her a kiss.

ลินดาหน้าแดงเมื่อจิมมีจูบเธอ

boil *(บอยล)* boiling, boiled

The water is boiling. Mother will switch the kettle off.

น้ำกำลังเดือด แม่จะปิดสวิตช์ของกา

borrow *(บ′อโร)* borrowing, borrowed

Helen is borrowing books

from the library.

เฮเลนกำลังยืมหนังสือจากห้องสมุด

bounce *(เบานซ)* bouncing, bounced

Andy is bouncing a ball.

แอนดีกำลังเลี้ยงลูกบอล

bow *(เบา)* bowing, bowed

The magician is bowing to the audience.

นักมายากลกำลังโค้งให้แก่ผู้ชม

box *(บ็อกซ)* boxing, boxed

That big boy boxed Andy on the chin.

เด็กโตคนนั้นชกแอนดีเข้าที่คาง

break *(บเรค)* breaking, broke

Willy broke the stick onto two pieces.

วิลลีหักไม้ออกเป็นสองท่อน

break down *(บเรค ดาวน)*

> Father's car broke down on his way to work.
>
> รถของพ่อเสียกลางทางระหว่างไปทำงาน

breathe *(บรีท)* breathing, breathed

> We breathe through our noses.
>
> เราหายใจผ่านทางจมูกของเรา

bring *(บริง)* bringing, brought

> Mother is bringing us some food.
>
> แม่กำลังนำอาหารมาให้เรา

brush *(บรัฌ)* brushing, brushed

> Jimmy is brushing his teeth, Kathy is brushing her hair.
>
> จิมมีกำลังแปรงฟันของเขา   แคธี กำลังแปรงผมของเธอ

build *(บิลด)* building, built

Peter is building a spaceship.

ปีเตอร์กำลังสร้างยานอวกาศ

bully *(บู'ลลิ)* bulling, bulled

That big boy is bullying the little children.

เด็กโตคนนั้นกำลังรังแกเด็ก ๆ

bump *(บัมพ)* bumping, bumped

Willy bumped onto a street lamp.

วิลลีชนเสาไฟ

burn *(เบิน)* burning, burnt

Father is burning some leaves.

พ่อกำลังเผาใบไม้

bury *(เบ'ริ)* burying, buried

That dog is burying a bone.

สุนัขกำลังฝังกระดูก

button *(บัททึน)* buttoning, buttoned

> Helen is buttoning up her jacket.
>
> เฮเลนกำลังกลัดกระดุมเสื้อแจ็คเก็ต ของเธอ

buy *(ไบ)* buying, bought

> Mandy is buying some flowers.
>
> แมนดีกำลังซื้อดอกไม้

C

call *(คอล)* calling, called

> Call the firemen to put out the fire.
>
> เรียกพนักงานดับเพลิงให้มาดับไฟ

call for *(คอล ฟอร)*

> Willy called for help when he

got into trouble while swimming.

วิลลีร้องเรียกให้คนช่วยเหลือเมื่อเขา
ได้รับความลำบากในขณะว่ายน้ำ

call off *(คอล ออฟ)*

The teacher had to call off the
picnic because it was raining.

ครูยกเลิกการไปปิกนิกเพราะฝนตก

camp *(แคมพ)* camping, camped

The scouts camped at the
beach.

ลูกเสือตั้งค่ายที่ชายหาด

care *(แค)* caring, cared

Simon cares for his pet rabbit.
He feeds it and cleans its cage
everyday.

ซิมอนดูแลกระต่ายของเขา เขาให้
อาหารและทำความสะอาดกรงของ

มันทุกวัน

carry *(แค่รี่)* carrying, carried

Mother is carrying the baby.

แม่กำลังอุ้มลูก

carry on *(แค่รี่ ออน)*

Grandmother let me carry on watching television although it was past my bedtime.

คุณยายอนุญาตให้ฉันดูโทรทัศน์ต่อ
ไปแม้ว่าเลยเวลานอนของฉันแล้ว

carve *(คาฝ)* carving, carved

Peter is carving a piece of wood onto a boat.

ปีเตอร์แกะสลักชิ้นไม้เป็นลำเรือ

catch *(แค็ช)* catching, caught

Jimmy held out both hands to catch the ball.

จิมมี่ใช้มือสองมือจับลูกบอล

celebrate *(เซ´ลอิบเรท)* celebrating, celebrated

Jane is celebrating her birthday by having a party.

เจนกำลังฉลองวันเกิดของเธอโดย
จัดงานเลี้ยง

change *(เชนจ)* changing, changed

Willy changed out of his wet
clothes into dry ones.

วิลลีเปลี่ยนเสื้อที่เปียกมาเป็นเสื้อผ้า
แห้ง

charge *(ชาจ)* charging, charged

The rhinoceros charged at the
fence.

แรดวิ่งเข้าใส่รั้ว

chase *(เชซ)* chasing, chased

The dogs chased that cat up a
tree.

สุนัขไล่แมวขึ้นบนต้นไม้

chat *(แช็ท)*   chatting, chatted

Kathy is chatting with her friend.

แคธี่กำลังพูดคุยกับเพื่อนของเธอ

cheat *(ชีท)*   cheating, cheated

Jimmy cheated at cards.

จิมมีโกงการเล่นไพ่

check *(เช็ค)*   checking, checked

Linda is counting her school books to check if she has them all.

ลินดานับหนังสือเรียนของเธอเพื่อตรวจดูว่ามันอยู่ครบหรือไม่

check in *(เช็ค อิน)*

We check in to the hotel at the start of our holiday.

เราลงชื่อเข้าพักโรงแรมในวันเริ่มต้นวันหยุด

check out *(เช็ค เอ๊าท)*

> We were sad to check out of the hotel at the end of our holiday.
>
> เรารู้สึกเสียใจที่จะต้องออกจากโรงแรมในวันสุดท้ายของวันหยุด

check up *(เช็ค อั๊พ)*

> We are going to see a movie to night, Simon is checking up on the times of the show.
>
> เราจะไปดูภาพยนตร์คืนนี้ ซิมมอน กำลังตรวจเวลาของการฉายอยู่

cheer *(เชีย)*   cheering, cheered

> The girls are cheering their team at the race.
>
> เด็ก ๆ ผู้หญิงกำลังเชียร์ทีมของตนในการแข่งขัน

cheer up *(เชีย อั๊พ)*

The cartoon show cheered up the children and made them laugh.

รายการการ์ตูนทำให้เด็ก ๆ มีความสุขและทำให้พวกเขาหัวเราะ

chew *(ชู)* chewing, chewed

The dog is chewing the bone.

สุนัขกำลังเคี้ยวกระดูก

chip *(ชิพ)* chipping, chipped

Andy dropped a plate and chipped it.

แอนดีทำจานตกและทำมันบิ่น

choose *(ชูส)* choosing, chose

It is hard to choose which sweets to buy when they all look so nice.

เป็นการยากที่จะเลือกซื้อขนมหวาน

เมื่อทุกอย่างดูน่ากินมาก

circle *(เซ′คคึล)* circling, circled

Helen is circling the right answer to the sum.

เฮเลนกำลังเขียนวงกลมรอบคำตอบของผลลัพธ์ที่ถูกต้อง

clap *(คแล็พ)* clapping, clapped

When the show ended, the children clapped their hands.

เด็กๆ พากันตบมือเมื่อการแสดงจบลง

clean *(คลีน)* cleaning, cleaned

Father cleans the car on Sundays.

พ่อทำความสะอาดรถทุกวันอาทิตย์

clean up *(คลีน อั๊พ)*

Mother told Jimmy to clean up his room.

แม่บอกให้จิมมีทำความสะอาดห้อง
ของเขา

clear *(คเลีย)* clearing, cleared

We will go out if the weather
clears.

เราจะออกไปเที่ยวถ้าอากาศปลอด
โปร่ง

clear away *(คเลีย อะ′เว)*

Kathy helps father clear away
the dishes after dinner.

แคธีช่วยพ่อยกจานออกไปหลังจาก
ทานอาหารเย็นแล้ว

clear off *(คเลีย อ็อฟ)*

The thief cleared off when he
saw a policeman coming.

ขโมยวิ่งหนีเมื่อเห็นตำรวจมา

clear out *(คเลีย เอ๊าท)*

Dad is clearing out the garage.

พ่อเก็บเข้าของออกจากโรงรถ (โยน
สิ่งของ)

climb *(ค ไลม)* climbing, climbed

The baby climbed up a chair.
ทารกปีนขึ้นบนเก้าอี้

clip *(คลิพ)* clipping, clipped

Mandy is clipping the papers
together so that they will not
get lost.
แมนดีกำลังหนีบกระดาษเข้าด้วยกัน
เพื่อไม่ให้มันหายไป

close *(คโลส)* closing, closed

Mother is closing the door.
แม่กำลังปิดประตู

cluck *(คลัค)* clucking, clucked

A hen clucked loudly after it
has laid some eggs.
แม่ไก่กะต๊ากหลังจากมันออกไข่แล้ว

coach *(โคช)*   coaching, coached

Mr. Thomson coaches the soccer team. He shows them how to kick the ball.

นายทอมสันผู้สอนทีมฟุตบอล เขาแสดงวิธีเตะบอลให้ลูกทีมดู

coil *(คอยล)*   coiling, coiled

Father coiled the garden hose after he had water the plants.

พ่อขดสายยางรดน้ำหลังจากรดน้ำต้นไม้เสร็จแล้ว

collapse *(ค็อลแล′พซ)*   collapsing, collapsed

The tent collapsed in the strong wind.

เต็นท์พังทลายด้วยกำลังลมที่รุนแรง

collect *(ค็อลเล็คท′)*   collecting, collected

Peter collects stamps from around the world.

ปีเตอร์สะสมแสตมป์ทั่วโลก

collide *(ค็อลไลด์)* colliding, collided

The car collided with a van.

รถยนต์ชนกับรถตู้

colour *(คัล'เออะ)* colouring, coloured

Andy is colouring a picture of a lion.

แอนดีกำลังระบายสีภาพสิงโต

comb *(โคม)* combing, combed

Jane is combing her long hair.

เจนกำลังหวีผมที่ยาวของเธอ

come *(คัม)* coming, came

Come with me. I'll show you the way.

มากับผม ผมจะบอกทางให้คุณ

  come across *(คัม อะครอส)*

Andy came across a gold chain while looking for his

lost marble.

แอนดีพบสร้อยคอทองคำโดยบัง-
เอิญขณะที่กำลังหาลูกหินของเขาที่
หายไป

come apart *(คัม อะพาท)*

The shirt was too small and came apart at the seam when Willy put it on.

เสื้อตัวเล็กมากและตะเข็บขาดเมื่อ
วิลลีสวมใส่

come back *(คัม แบ็ค)*

Boomerangs always come back when thrown.

บุมมาแรงจะย้อนกลับมาที่เดิมเสมอ
เมื่อขว้างออกไป

come off *(คัม ออฟ)*

A button came off Kathy's coat.

เสื้อโค้ทของแคธีกระดุมขาด

come on *(คัม ออน)*

The magician came on the
stage wearing a long black
cape.

นักมายากลขึ้นมาบนเวทีสวมหมวก
สีดำทรงสูง

come out *(คัม เอ๊าท)*

The moon and the star come
out at night.

พระจันทร์และดวงดาวออกมาใน
เวลากลางคืน

compare *(ค็อมแพร์')* comparing, compared

Benny is tall compared with
Helen.

เบนนีสูงเมื่อเปรียบเทียบกับเฮเลน

complain *(ค็อมพเลน')*

complaining, complained

Kathy complained to mother that Andy had torn her book.

แคธีฟ้องแม่ว่าแอนดีฉีกหนังสือของเธอ

confuse *(ค็อนฟยูส′)* confusing, confused

The signs confused the driver.

เครื่องหมายทำให้คนขับรถสับสน

congratulate *(ค็อนกแร′ชอิวเลท)*

congratulating, congratulated

Everyone congratulated the winner.

ทุกคนแสดงความยินดีกับผู้ชนะ

connect *(ค็อนเนค′ท)* connecting, connected

Uncle Roy connected the aerial to the television.

ลุงรอยต่อสายอากาศเข้ากับเครื่องรับโทรทัศน์

consider *(ค็อนซิด'เออะ)*

considering, considered

Mother and father are considering what to get for Kathy
for her birthday.

แม่และพ่อกำลังพิจารณาว่าจะให้
อะไรแก่แคธีเพื่อเป็นของขวัญวันเกิด

consist *(ค็อนซีซ'ท)* consisting, consisted

This gift set consists of two
story books and two tapes.

ชุดของขวัญประกอบด้วยหนังสือ
นิทาน 2 เล่ม และเทปสองม้วน

construct *(ค็อนสทรัคท')*

constructing, constructed

Peter constructed a spaceship
from clothes peg.

ปีเตอร์สร้างยานอวกาศด้วยหมุดปัก
ผ้า

contain *(ค็อนเทน´)* containing, contained

This bottle contains ink.

ขวดบรรจุด้วยหมึก

continue *(ค็อนทีน´ยู)* continuing, continued

Mother, don't stop now. Please continue reading the story, the children asked.

แม่ อย่าเพิ่งหยุดตอนนี้ กรุณาอ่านนิทานต่อไป ลูก ๆ ขอร้อง

contribute *(ค็อนทริบ´อิวท)*

contributing, contributed

The children contributed some money to buy a present for their mother.

ลูก ๆ เรี่ยไรเงินกันเพื่อซื้อของขวัญให้แม่ของพวกเขา

control *(ค็อนโทรล´)* controlling, controlled

Andy controls the robot by

remote control.

แคนดีบังคับหุ่นยนต์โดยใช้รีโมท
คอนโทรลบังคับ

cook *(คุค)*   cooking, cooked

Mother cooked a delicious
roast chicken.

แม่ปรุงไก่ย่างอร่อย

cool *(คูล)*   cooling, cooled

Mandy is cooling her feet in
the stream.

แมนดีเอาเท้าแช่ลงในลำธาร

cool down *(คูล ดาวน)*

The porridge was hot, so the
three bears left it to cool
down.

ข้าวต้มข้าวโอ๊ตร้อน ดังนั้นเจ้าหมี
สามตัวปล่อยให้มันเย็นลง

cool off *(คูล ออฟ)*

> The children felt hot, so they jumped into the water to cool off.
>
> เด็กๆ รู้สึกร้อน ดังนั้นพวกเขากระ-โดดลงในน้ำเพื่อให้เย็น

copy *(คอพ′อิ)* copying, copied

> Linda copied the sums from the blackboard.
>
> ลินดาคัดลอกผลลัพธ์ของโจทย์เลขจากกระดานดำ

cost *(ค็อซท)* costing, cost

> This hamburger costs $ 1.30.
>
> แฮมเบอร์เกอร์ราคา 1.30 เหรียญ

cough *(ค็อฟ)* coughing, coughed

> Willy coughed because he had a sore throat.
>
> วิลลีไอเพราะว่าเขาเจ็บคอ

count *(เคานท)*   counting, counted

> The rich man is counting his money.

> ชายผู้ร่ำรวยกำลังนับเงินของเขา

cover *(คัฝเออะ)*   covering, covered

> Kathy covered her face with her hands.

> แคธีเอามือปิดหน้าของเธอ

  cover up *(คัฝเออะ อั๊พ)*

> Andy covered up the ink stain so his mother would not see it.

> แอนดีปกปิดรอยเปื้อนหมึก   เพื่อที่ แม่จะได้มองไม่เห็น

crack *(คแร็ค)*   cracking, cracked

> The vase cracked when it was dropped.

> แจกันแตกเมื่อมันตกลงมา

crash *(คแร็ฌ)* crashing, crashed

The car crashed into the wall.

รถยนต์ชนเข้ากับกำแพง

crawl *(ครอล)* crawling, crawled

The baby is crawling across the room.

ทารกกำลังคลานผ่านห้อง

create *(คริเอท′)* creating, created

The magician created a monster with his spells.

นักมายากลสร้างสัตว์ประหลาดด้วยมนต์ของเขา

creep *(ครีพ)* creeping, crept

Jimmy crept up behind Linda to frighten her.

จิมมีค่อย ๆ ย่องเข้ามาข้างหลังลินดาเพื่อทำให้เธอตกใจ

croak *(คโรค)* croaking, croaked

The frogs are croaking a song.

กบกำลังส่งเสียงร้องเพลง

cross *(คร็อซ)* crossing, crossed

We looked left and right before crossing the street.

เรามองซ้ายและขวาก่อนข้ามถนน

cross-out *(คร็อซ เอ๊าท)*

Peter crossed out a mistake in his book.

ปีเตอร์ขีดฆ่าข้อผิดพลาดในหนังสือ ของเขา

crouch *(คเราช)* crouching, crouched

Kathy crouched behind a chair to hide from Willy.

แคธีหมอบหลังเก้าอี้เพื่อแอบซ่อน วิลลี

crow *(คโร)* crowing, crowed

The rooster crows loudly in the early morning.

ไก่ตัวผู้ขันเสียงดังในเวลาเช้าตรู่

crowd *(คเราด)* crowding, crowded

The children are crowding around the friendly chimpanzee.

เด็กๆ กำลังรุมล้อมลิงชิมแพนซีที่เป็นมิตร

crumble *(ครัม'บึล)* crumbling, crumbled

Mother is crumbling the biscuit into a bowl.

แม่กำลังบี้ขนมปังกรอบลงในชามอ่าง

crumple *(ครัม'พึล)* crumpling, crumpled

Andy crumpled up the drawing.

แอนดีขยำภาพเขียน

crush *(ครัฌ)* crushing, crushed

The steamroller crushed the soccer ball.

รถบดสนามฟุตบอล

cuddle *(คัด′ดึล)* cuddling, cuddled

The baby is cuddling a teddy bear.

ทารกกำลังกอดตุ๊กตาหมี

curl *(เคิล)* curling, curled

The cat curled up on the cushion.

แมวขดตัวอยู่บนเบาะ

curtsy *(เคิทซี)* curtsying, curtsied

Cinderella curtsied to the queen.

ซินเดอเรลลาถอนสายบัวต่อพระพักตร์ราชินี

cut *(คัท)* cutting, cut

>Aunt Molly is cutting the cake into slices.
>
>ป้ามอลลีกำลังตัดเค้กเป็นชิ้น ๆ

cut down *(คัท ดาวน)*

>Father cut down a tree in the garden.
>
>พ่อตัดต้นไม้ในสวน

cut off *(คัท ออฟ)*

>Bobby is cutting off the sleeves from his T-shirt.
>
>บ็อบบีกำลังตัดแขนเสื้อออกจากเสื้อยืดของเขา

cut out *(คัท เอ๊าท)*

>Linda is cutting out pictures from a magazine.
>
>ลินดากำลังตัดรูปภาพจากนิตยสาร

cut up *(คัท อัพ)*

> Kathy cuts up the vegetables to make a salad.
>
> แคธีหั่นผักเพื่อทำสลัด

cycle *(ไซเคิล)* cycling, cycled

> Bobby cycles home from school.
>
> บ็อบบีถีบจักรยานจากโรงเรียนมาบ้าน

D

damage *(แดมอิจ)* damaging, damaged

> The ship was damaged when it hit the rocks.
>
> เรือเสียหายเมื่อมันแล่นชนโขดหิน

dance *(ดานซ)* dancing, danced

> The children are dancing hap-

pily round the Christmas tree.

เด็กๆ กำลังเต้นกันอย่างสนุกสนาน

รอบต้นคริสต์มาส

darn *(ดาน)* darning, darned

Mother is darning a hole in

Jimmy's sock.

แม่กำลังชุนรอยโหว่ถุงเท้าของจิมมี

dash *(แด็ฌ)* dashing, dashed

The dog dashed across the

street.

สุนัขพุ่งตัวข้ามถนน

deal *(ดีล)* dealing, dealt

You deal all the cards to play

snap.

คุณแจกไพ่เพื่อเล่นสแนพ *(ไพ่ชนิด*

หนึ่งเล่นกันหลายคน)

decide *(ดีไซด′)* deciding, decided

Helen could not decide

whether to wear shorts or a
dress.

เฮเลนไม่สามารถตัดสินใจได้ว่าจะนุ่ง
กางเกงขาสั้นหรือแต่งชุดดี

decorate *(เดคโอะเรท)* decorating, decorated

Mandy is decorating the hall.

แมนดีกำลังตกแต่งห้องโถง

defend *(ดิเฟนด์)* defending, defended

The soldiers are defending
their country from attack.

เหล่าทหารกำลังป้องกันประเทศจาก
การโจมตี

delight *(ดิไลท์)* delighting, delighted

Jane was delighted with her
new puppy.

เจนมีความสุขกับลูกสุนัขตัวใหม่ของ
เธอ

deliver *(ดิลีฝเออะ)* delivering, delivered

The postman delivered a parcel to Linda's house.

บุรุษไปรษณีย์ส่งพัสดุภัณฑ์ที่บ้านของลินดา

demand *(ดิมานด์)* demanding, demanded

The spoilt child demanded the biggest ice-cream.

เด็กที่ถูกตามใจต้องการไอศกรีมก้อนใหญ่ที่สุด

demonstrate *(เด่มอันซทเรท)*

demonstrating, demonstrated

The fireman demonstrated how to put out the fire.

พนักงานดับเพลิงสาธิตวิธีการดับไฟ

describe *(ดิซไคร์บ)* describing, described

Jimmy is describing to the policeman that dog that he

has lost.

จิมมีกำลังอธิบายให้ตำรวจฟังเกี่ยว
กับสุนัขที่หายไป

deserve *(ดิเสิฝ)* deserving, deserved

Bobby practised hard for the
swimming contest and
deserved first prize.

บ็อบบีฝึกว่ายน้ำอย่างหนักเพื่อแข่ง
ขันการว่ายน้ำและได้รับรางวัลที่ ๑

design *(ดีไสน์)* designing, designed

Aunt Molly is designing a
party dress for Kathy.

ป้ามอลลีกำลังออกแบบชุดงานเลี้ยง
ให้แก่แคธี

destroy *(ดิซทรอย์)* destroying, destroyed

The big boy destroyed Andy's
sandcastle.

เด็กโตคนนั้นทำลายปราสาททราย

ของแอนดี

develop *(ดิเฝล'อัพ)* developing, developed

The bodybuilder developed huge muscles.

นักเล่นกล้ามพัฒนากล้ามให้ใหญ่โต

dial *(ได'แอ็ล)* dialing, dialed

Helen dialed 999 to call the police.

เฮเลนหมุนหมายเลข 999 เพื่อเรียกตำรวจ

die *(ได)* dying, died

The bear died after the hunter shot it.

หมีตายหลังจากนายพรานยิงมัน

die away *(ได อะเว)*

The music died away at the end of the song.

ดนตรีแผ่วลงในตอนท้ายของเพลง

die down *(ได ดาวน)*

We let the fire die down after the barbecue.

เราปล่อยให้ไฟมอดหลังจากที่เราย่าง บาบีคิวแล้ว

dig *(ดิก)* digging, dug

Uncle Roy is digging a hole to plant the tree.

ลุงรอยกำลังขุดหลุมเพื่อปลูกต้นไม้

dip *(ดิพ)* dipping, dipped

The cat dipped its paw into the fish tank to try to catch a fish.

แมวล้วงอุ้งเท้าของมันลงในตู้ปลา เพื่อพยายามจับปลา

direct *(ดิเรคท′)* directing, directed

The policeman is directing the traffic at the crossroads.

ตำรวจกำลังอำนวยการการจราจร
ที่ทางแยก

disappear *(ดิแซ็พเพีย′)*

disappearing, dsappeared

The wizard disappeared in a
puff of smoke.

พ่อมดหายตัวไปในกลุ่มควัน

discover *(ดิซคัฟเออะ)*

discovering, discovered

The scientist discovered a
new plant in the forest.

นักวิทยาศาสตร์ค้นพบพืชใหม่ในป่า

discuss *(ดิซคัซ′)* discussing, discussed

Willy, Linda and Jimmy discussed where they wanted to
go for a picnic.

วิลลี ลินดา และจิมมี ปรึกษากันถึง
สถานที่ที่พวกเขาจะไปปิกนิก

disguise *(ดิซไกส์)* disguising, disguised

The thief disguised himself as
an old lady.
โจรปลอมตัวเป็นหญิงชรา

dislike *(ดิซไลค์)* disliking, disliked

Andy dislikes vegetables.
แอนดี้ไม่ชอบผัก

dismiss *(ดิซมีซ์)* dismissing, dismissed

At the end of the day the children are dismissed from class.
ช่วงท้ายของวัน เด็ก ๆ ได้รับอนุญาต
ให้ออกจากชั้นเรียนได้

display *(ดิซพเล่)* displaying, displayed

The new books are displayed
in the shop window.
หนังสือใหม่แสดงไว้ในตู้โชว์ของร้าน

disturb *(ดิซเทิบ)* disturbing, disturbed

Do not disturb Dad. He is

sleeping.

อย่ารบกวนพ่อ พ่อกำลังหลับอยู่

dive *(ไดฟ์)* diving, dived

Bobby is diving into the pool.

บ็อบบีกำลังดำลงไปในสระน้ำ

divide *(ดิไฟด์')* dividing, divided

Jimmy is dividing the sweets into two equal piles.

จิมมีกำลังแบ่งขนมหวานออกเป็น 2 กองเท่า ๆ กัน

do *(ดู)* doing, did

Jimmy must do his home-work. He cannot play with Andy now.

จิมต้องทำการบ้าน เขาไม่สามารถเล่นกับแอนดีได้ในตอนนี้

do away *(ดู อะเว)*

Jack did away with the giant.

แจ๊คกำจัดยักษ์

do up *(ดู คั๊พ)*

> Bobby did up an old bike.
> Now it looks like new.
> บ็อบบีทำความสะอาดรถจักรยาน
> คันเก่าของเขาแล้ว   ตอนนี้มันดู
> เหมือนจักรยานใหม่เลย

dock *(ด็อค)*   docking, docked

> The ship docked at the wharf
> to unload its cargo.
> เรือเทียบท่าเพื่อขนสินค้าลง

donate *(โด′เนท)*   donating, donated

> Mandy donated her savings
> to the old folk's home.
> แมนดีบริจาคเงินที่เธอเก็บไว้ให้กับ
> บ้านคนชรา

doodle *(ดู′ดึล)*   doodling, doodled

> Helen is doodling on a piece

of paper.

เฮเลนขีดเส้นขยุกขยิกบนกระดาษ

doze *(โดส)* dozing, dozed

Dogs love to doze in the sun.

สุนัขชอบนอนตากแดด

drag *(ดแร็ก)* dragging, dragged

The men are dragging the boat up onto the beach.

ชายคนนั้นกำลังลากเรือขึ้นมาบนชายหาด

drain *(ดเรน)* draining, drained

Kathy let the dishes drain after she washed them.

แคธีปล่อยให้จานสะเด็ดน้ำหลังจากล้างเสร็จแล้ว

draw *(ดรอ)* drawing, drew

Andy is drawing a rabbit.

แอนดีกำลังวาดภาพกระต่าย

dream *(ดรีม)* dreaming, dreamed or dreamt
Helen dreams of being a pilot.
เฮเลนฝันจะเป็นนักบิน

dress *(ดเรซ)* dressing, dressed
Linda dressed as a witch for
Halloween.
ลินดาแต่งตัวเป็นแม่มดในวันฮอล-
ลอวีน

drift *(ดริฟท)* drifting, drifted
There was no wind and the
boat drifted on the sea.
ไม่มีลมและเรือก็ลอยอยู่ในทะเล

drill *(ดริล)* drilling, drilled
Uncle Roy is drilling a hole in
the wall.
ลุงรอยกำลังเจาะรูบนผนัง

drink *(ดริงค)* drinking, drank
Willy drank a glass of milk

with breakfast.

วิลลี่ดื่มนม ๑ แก้วกับอาหารเช้า

drink up *(ดริงค อัพ)*

The elephant drank up all the water in the bucket.

ช้างดื่มน้ำที่อยู่ในถังหมด

drip *(ดริพ)* dripping, dripped

Water is dripping from the ceiling onto the floor.

น้ำกำลังหยดจากเพดานลงบนพื้น

drive *(ดไรฝ)* driving, drove

Father drives the car to work each morning.

พ่อขับรถไปทำงานทุกเช้า

drop *(ดร็อพ)* dropping, dropped

Linda dropped an egg on the floor.

ลินดาทำไข่ตกลงบนพื้น

drop in *(ดร็อพ อิน)*

>Andy dropped in to see his grandmother.
>
>แอนดีแวะเยี่ยมคุณยายของเขา

drop off *(ดร็อพ ออฟ)*

>Mother dropped Kathy off at school.
>
>แม่ส่งแคธีที่โรงเรียน

drown *(ดเราน)* drowning, drowned

>The lifeguard rescued Willy who was drowning.
>
>เจ้าหน้าที่ไลฟ์การ์ดช่วยเหลือวิลลีที่กำลังจมน้ำ

dry *(ดไร)* drying, dried

>After a bath, you dry yourself well with a towel.
>
>หลังจากอาบน้ำเสร็จแล้ว คุณเช็ดตัวด้วยผ้าเช็ดตัว

dry out *(ดไร เอ๊าท)*

> The puddle dried out in the hot sun.
>
> ดินแตกระแหงภายใต้แสงอาทิตย์ร้อนจัด

duck *(ดัค)* ducking, ducked

> The giant ducked his head to get through the door.
>
> ยักษ์ก้มศีรษะเพื่อลอดประตูออกไป

dump *(ดัมพ)* dumping, dumped

> The truck dumped the rubbish in a head.
>
> รถบรรทุกเทขยะใส่ศีรษะ

dust *(ดัซท)* dusting, dusted

> Mother is dusting the furniture.
>
> แม่กำลังปัดฝุ่นที่เฟอร์นิเจอร์

E

earn *(เอิน)* earning, earned

Bobby earns pocket money by washing cars.

บ็อบบีหาเงินโดยการล้างรถ

eat *(อีท)* eating, ate

Elephants eat a lot.

ช้างกินอาหารมาก

eat up *(อีท อัพ)*

The mouse ate up all the cheese.

หนูกินเนยแข็งหมด

edge *(เอ็จ)* edging, edged

The clown edged his way carefully along the narrow plank.

ตัวตลกค่อย ๆ เคลื่อนตัวอย่างระมัด

ระวังไปตามกระดานแคบ ๆ

elect *(อิเลคท')* electing, elected

The team elected the captain from among themselves.

ผู้เล่นในทีมเลือกหัวหน้าทีมจาก
คนในกลุ่มของพวกเขาเอง

embarrass *(เอ็มแบ'แร็ซ)*

embarrassing, embarrassed

Andy embarrassed his father by being rude in front of Aunt Molly.

แอนดีทำให้พ่อของเขาขายหน้าโดย
การใช้วาจาหยาบคายต่อหน้าป้า
มอลลี

embrace *(เอ็มบเรซ')* embracing, embraced

Father embraced mother lov-ingly.

พ่อสวมกอดแม่อย่างรักใคร่

emerge *(อิเมิจ')* emerging, emerged

> Suddenly a shark cmerged from the water.
>
> ทันใดนั้นปลาฉลามก็โผล่มาจากน้ำ

employ *(เอ็มพลอย')* employing, employed

> Sam is employing to clean windows.
>
> แซมใช้เวลาทำความสะอาดหน้าต่าง

empty *(เอม'ทิ)* emptying, emptied

> The baby emptied the box of blocks onto the floor.
>
> เด็กคนนั้นเทกล่องตัวต่อของเล่นลงบนพื้นจนหมด

end *(เอ็นด)* ending, ended

> The road ends at the cliff edge.
>
> ถนนไปสุดที่ริมหน้าผา

engrave *(เอ็นกเรฝ)* engraving, engraved

Andy is engraving his name in the tree trunk.

แอนดีกำลังจารึกชื่อของเขาบนต้นไม้

enjoy *(เอ็นจอย´)* enjoying, enjoyed

Mandy enjoys watching television.

แมนดีเพลิดเพลินกับการดูโทรทัศน์

enter *(เอน´เทอะ)* entering, entered

The burglar is entering the house by the window.

โจรกำลังปีนเข้าบ้านจากทางหน้าต่าง

entertain *(เอน´เทอะเทน´)*

entertaining, entertained

The clown entertained us with his funny tricks.

ตัวตลกต้อนรับเราด้วยกลที่ขบขัน

equal *(อีค'แวล)* equalling, equalled

$$1 + 1 = 2$$

One and one equals two.

หนึ่งบวกหนึ่งเท่ากับสอง

erase *(อิเรซ')* erasing, erased

It is easy to erase mistakes with a rubber.

เป็นการง่ายที่จะลบข้อผิดพลาดด้วยยางลบ

escape *(เอ็สเคพ')* escaping, escaped

The monkey escaped from the cage.

ลิงหนีออกจากกรง

examine *(เอ็กแสม'อิน)*

examining, examined

The doctor is examining the sick boy.

หมอกำลังตรวจเด็กผู้ชายที่ป่วย

exchange *(เอ็คซเชนจ์)*

exchanging, exchanged

Willy is exchanging shorts with Peter.

วิลลีแลกกางเกงขาสั้นกับปีเตอร์

excite *(เอ็คไซท์)* exciting, excited

Mandy was excited when she saw the gold cup.

แมนดีตื่นเต้นเมื่อเธอเห็นถ้วยทอง

excuse *(เอ็คซคยูซ์)* excusing, excused

Jane is excused from sports because she hurts her ankles.

เจนได้รับอนุญาตให้หยุดเล่นกีฬา เพราะว่าเธอบาดเจ็บที่ข้อเท้า

exercise *(เอค์เซอะไซส)* exercising, exercised

Bobby exercises everyday to keep fit.

บ็อบบีออกกำลังกายทุกวันเพื่อให้

ร่างกายสมบูรณ์

expand *(เอ็คซแพนด′)* expanding, expanded

A balloon expands when you blow it up.

ลูกโป่งขยายออกเมื่อคุณเป่ามัน

expect *(เอ็คซเพคท′)* expecting, expected

I expect it will rain today. There are a lot of dark clouds in the sky.

ฉันคาดว่าวันนี้ฝนจะตก บนท้องฟ้า มีแต่เมฆฝน

explain *(เอ็คซพเลน′)* explaining, explained

The teacher explained to the student how to jump over the hurdles.

ครูอธิบายวิธีกระโดดข้ามรั้วให้นัก เรียนฟัง

explore *(เอ็คซพโล′)* exploring, explored

Kathy is exploring the rock pool looking for the crabs.

แคธีกำลังสำรวจแอ่งหินมองหาปู

F

face *(เฟซ)* facing, faced

Linda faced the clock to see what time it was.

ลินดาหมุนนาฬิกามาดูว่าเวลาเท่าไร

face up *(เฟซ อัพ)*

It is hard to face up to your teacher when you have not done your homework.

เป็นการยากที่จะเผชิญหน้ากับครู เมื่อคุณทำการบ้านไม่เสร็จ

fade *(เฟด)* fading, faded

> The curtains have faded.
> ม่านสีซีดลง

fail *(เฟล)* failing, failed

> Bobby failed to clear the high jump.
> บ็อบบีกระโดดสูงไม่พ้น

faint *(เฟนท)* fainting, fainted

> Mandy saw a ghost and faint.
> แมนดีเห็นผีและเป็นลม

fake *(เฟค)* faking, faked

> Andy faked a stomachache because he did not want to go to school.
> แอนดีแกล้งทำเป็นปวดท้องเพราะเขาไม่อยากไปโรงเรียน

fall *(ฟอล)* falling, fell

> Willy tripped over a stone and

fell on his hands and knees.

วิลลีสะดุดก้อนหินและล้มพังพาบ

fall off *(ฟอล ออฟ)*

Andy fell off his chair in fright.

แอนดีตกจากเก้าอี้ด้วยความตกใจ

fan *(แฟน)* fanning, fanned

Aunt Molly fanned herself to keep cool.

ป้ามอลลีพัดตัวเธอเองเพื่อให้เย็น

farm *(ฟาม)* farming, farmed

Uncle Roy farms a small piece of land behind the house.

ลุงรอยทำฟาร์มเล็ก ๆ หลังบ้าน

fast *(ฟัซท)* fasting, fasted

The holy man is fasting. He is not eating any food.

ชายที่น่าเคารพอดอาหาร   เขาไม่

ยอมกินอะไรเลย

fasten *(ฟา'ซึน)* fastening, fastened

Willy is fastening his seat belt.
วิลลีคาดเข็มขัดนิรภัยที่นั่งของเขา

fear *(เฟีย)* fearing, feared

Kathy fears snakes.
แคธีกลัวงู

feed *(ฟีด)* feeding, fed

Simon feeds his pet rabbit
carrots and lettuce.
ซิมมอนเลี้ยงกระต่ายด้วยหัวแครอท
และผักกาดหอม

feel *(ฟีล)* feeling, felt

Rabbits feel soft and cuddly.
กระต่ายให้ความรู้สึกนิ่มและน่ากอด

feel like *(ฟีล ไลค)*

On a hot day we feel like a
cold drink.

ในวันที่อากาศร้อนเรารู้สึกอยากได้
เครื่องดื่มเย็นๆ

fence *(เฟ็นซ)* fencing, fenced

Uncle Roy is fencing the tree
with wire.

ลุงรอยกำลังทำรั้วลวดหนามล้อม
รอบต้นไม้

fetch *(เฟ็ช)* fetching, fetched

The dog fetches the stick for
Jimmy.

สุนัขคาบไม้มาให้จิมมี

fight *(ไฟท)* fighting, fought

Bobby and Jimmy are fighting.

บ็อบบีและจิมมีกำลังทะเลาะกัน

fill *(ฟิล)* filling, filled

Andy is filling the pool with
water.

แอนดีกำลังเติมน้ำลงในสระน้ำ

fill up *(ฟิล อัพ)*

Jane filled up the bucket with sand.

เจนเติมทรายลงในถัง

film *(ฟิลม)* filming, filmed

They are filming a fight.

เขากำลังถ่ายภาพยนตร์การต่อสู้

find *(ไฟนด)* finding, found

Mandy found a coin on the footpath.

แมนดีพบเหรียญบนทางเท้า

find out *(ไฟนด เอ๊าท)*

Jimmy looked in the phone book to find out Peter's phone number.

จิมมีดูในสมุดโทรศัพท์เพื่อหาเบอร์ โทรศัพท์ของปีเตอร์

finish *(ฟีน′อิฌ)* finishing, finished

The rabbit finished first in the race.

กระต่ายชนะการวิ่งแข่งขัน

finish with *(ฟีน′อิฌ วิธ)*

Helen had finished with the book, so she returned it to the library.

เฮเลนอ่านหนังสือจบแล้ว ดังนั้นเธอจึงส่งคืนห้องสมุด

fire *(ไฟร)* firing, fired

The hunter is firing at the birds.

นักล่าสัตว์กำลังยิงนก

fish *(ฟีฌ)* fishing, fished

Jimmy likes to fish with his father.

จิมมีชอบตกปลากับพ่อของเขา

fit *(ฟิท)* fitting, fitted

Cinderclla's foot fitted the shoe perfectly.

เท้าของซิลเดอเรลลาขนาดเหมาะกับรองเท้าพอดี

fit in *(ฟิท อิน)*

Only five people could fit in the car.

รถคันนี้นั่งได้ห้าคนเท่านั้น

fix *(ฟิคซ)* fixing, fixed

Helen is fixing lunch.

เฮเลนกำลังเตรียมอาหารเที่ยง

fizz *(ฟิส)* fizzing, fizzed

This drink fizzed for a while when I pour it out.

เครื่องดื่มนี้เป็นฟองอยู่ครู่หนึ่งเมื่อฉันรินมันออกมา

flag *(ฟแล็ก)* flagging, flagged

The people flag the build-ings to celebrate the king's birth-day.

ผู้คนติดธงเพื่อฉลองวันพระราชสม–ภพของพระมหากษัตริย์

flag down *(ฟแล็ก ดาวน)*

We flag down a taxi.

เขาโบกแท็กซี่ให้จอด

flap *(ฟแล็พ)* flapping, flapped

The washing is flapping in the wind.

ผ้าที่ซักแล้วกำลังโบกสะบัดไปตามลม

flash *(ฟแล็ฌ)* flashing, flashed

The light from the lighthouse flashed across the sea.

แสงจากประภาคารส่องแสงข้ามทะเล

flatten *(ฟแลท'ทึน)* flattening, flattened

>Willy flattened the plasticine.
>
>วิลลีนวดดินน้ำมัน

flee *(ฟลี)* fleeing, fled

>The animal are fleeing from the burning forest.
>
>สัตว์กำลังวิ่งหนีจากไฟไหม้ป่า

flick *(ฟลิค)* flicking, flicked

>The cow is flicking the flies with its tail.
>
>วัวใช้หางปัดแมลงวัน

fling *(ฟลิง)* flinging, flung

>The lazy boy flung his clothes on the floor.
>
>เด็กขี้เกียจเหวี่ยงเสื้อของเขาลงบนพื้น

flip *(ฟลิพ)* flipping, flipped

>I can flip a coin in the air.

ผมสามารถดีดเหรียญขึ้นในอากาศ

flit *(ฟลิท)* flitting, flitted

The butterfly flits from flower to flower.

ผีเสื้อบินโผจากดอกไม้ดอกหนึ่งไป
อีกดอกหนึ่ง

float *(ฟโลท)* floating, floated

Kathy can float on her back.

แคธีสามารถนอนหงายลอยตัวบน
น้ำได้

flood *(ฟลัด)* flooding, flooded

Andy left the tap on and
flooded the floor.

แอนดีเปิดก๊อกน้ำทิ้งไว้และทำให้น้ำ
ท่วมพื้น

flow *(ฟโล)* flowing, flowed

The river flows down to th sea.

แม่น้ำไหลลงสู่ทะเล

fluff *(ฟลัฟ)* fluffing, fluffed

> The hen is fluffing out its feathers.
> แม่ไก่กำลังสลัดขนของมัน

flush *(ฟลัฌ)* flushing, flushed

> Jane is flushing the toilet.
> เจนกำลังกดน้ำในห้องสุขา

fly *(ฟไล)* flying, flew

> Birds fly in the sky.
> นกบินในอากาศ

foam *(โฟม)* foaming, foamed

> The beer foams over the glass.
> ฟองเบียร์ล้นแก้ว

fold *(โฟลด)* folding, folded

> Andy folded a piece of paper to make a dart.
> แอนดีพับเศษกระดาษเพื่อทำลูกดอก

follow *(ฟอล'โล)* following, followed

The dog followed Jimmy home from school.

สุนัขเดินตามจิมมีจากโรงเรียนกลับบ้าน

forget *(เฟาะเกท')* forgetting, forgot

Poor Willy cannot write. He has forgotten to bring his pencil.

วิลลีผู้น่าสงสารไม่สามารถเขียนได้ เพราะเขาลืมดินสอ

form *(ฟอม)* forming, formed

Jimmy forms a K with his body.

จิมมีทำรูปตัว K ด้วยลำตัวของเขา

free *(ฟรี)* freeing, freed

Linda is freeing the bird from its cage.

ลินดาปล่อยนกออกจากกรง

freeze *(ฟรีส)* freezing, froze

When water freezes it becomes ice.

เมื่อน้ำถึงจุดแข็งมันจะกลายเป็นน้ำแข็ง

frighten *(ฟไร'ทึน)* frightening, frightened

Little Miss Muffed was frightened by the spider.

คุณมัพพ์ตัวน้อยกลัวแมงมุม

frown *(ฟเราน)* frowning, frowned

Bobby frowns when he is worry.

บ็อบบี้ทำหน้านิ่วคิ้วขมวดเมื่อเขารู้สึกเป็นกังวล

fry *(ฟไร)* frying, fried

Mother is frying an egg for Andy.

แม่กำลังทอดไข่ให้แอนดี

furnish *(เฟอนิฌ)* furnishing, furnished

Aunt Molly furnished her room with a bed, dressing table and chair.

ป้ามอลลีจัดห้องของเธอด้วยเตียงนอน โต๊ะเครื่องแป้ง และเก้าอี้

G

gallop *(แกล′ลัพ)* galloping, galloped

Jimmy was afraid when his horse galloped down the hill.

จิมมีตกใจกลัวเมื่อม้าควบลงจากเนินเขา

gamble *(แกม′บึล)* gambling, gambled

These men are gambling.

ชายเหล่านี้กำลังเล่นการพนัน

garden *(ก่าดึน)* gardening, gardened

Father is gardening. He is planting roses.

พ่อกำลังทำสวน　　เขากำลังปลูกกุหลาบ

gasp *(กาซพ)* gasping, gasped

The water was so cold, Bobby gasped with shock.

น้ำเย็นมาก　บ็อบบีอ้าปากค้างด้วยความตกใจ

gather *(แกท'เออะ)* gathering, gathered

Grandfather gathered fruit from the trees.

คุณตาเก็บผลไม้จากต้น

gaze *(เกส)* gazing, gazed

Kathy is gazing at the stars.

แคธีกำลังเพ่งดูดาว

get *(เก็ท)* getting, got

Jimmy got a pail of water from the river.

จิมมีนำถังน้ำมาจากแม่น้ำ

get across *(เก็ท อะครอซ)*

Jimmy got across the river on a bridge.

จิมมีข้ามแม่น้ำมาบนสะพาน

get along *(เก็ท อะลอง)*

Helen is a sweet girl who gets along with all her classmates.

เฮเลนเป็นเด็กหญิงที่น่ารัก เธอเข้ากับเพื่อนร่วมห้องทุกคนได้ดี

get around *(เก็ท อะราวด)*

Pilots get around a lot. They visit many countries.

นักบินเดินทางไปทั่ว พวกเขาไปมาหลายประเทศ

get at *(เก็ท แอ็ท)*

> Andy cannot get at the bird.
> แอนดีไม่สามารถจับนกได้

get away *(เก็ท อะเว)*

> Get away from the fire! You might. get hurt.
> ถอยให้ห่างจากไฟ คุณอาจได้รับ
> อันตราย

get back *(เก็ท แบ็ค)*

> The runners were tired when they got back from the cross-country run.
> นักวิ่งต่างก็เหนื่อยล้าเมื่อพวกเขา
> กลับมาจากวิ่งวิบาก

get down *(เก็ท ดาวน)*

> Simon climbed a tree and couldn't get down.
> ซิมอนปีนขึ้นต้นไม้และไม่สามารถ

ลงมาได้

get dressed *(เก็ท ดเรซ)*

It is late. You must get dressed at once.

สายแล้ว คุณต้องแต่งตัวเดี๋ยวนี้

get in *(เก็ท อิน)*

Ali Baba got in a jar to hide from the thieves.

อลี บาบา เข้าไปอยู่ในโอ่งเพื่อหลบ ซ่อนโจร

get into *(เก็ท อินทู)*

Father got into the car and drove off.

พ่อขึ้นรถและขับออกไป

get off *(เก็ท ออฟ)*

Bobby got off the bus at the swimming pool.

บ็อบบีลงรถประจำทางที่สระว่ายน้ำ

get on *(เก็ท ออน)*

Linda got on the horse without any help.

ลินดาขึ้นขี่ม้าโดยปราศจากการช่วยเหลือใด ๆ

get over *(เก็ท โอ'เฝอะ)*

Peter couldn't get over the wall.

ปีเตอร์ไม่สามารถข้ามกำแพงได้

get up *(เก็ท อัพ)*

Andy gets up at 7 o'clock.

แอนดีตื่นนอนเวลา 7 นาฬิกา

giggle *(กิก'กึล)* giggling, giggled

The playful puppy made Kathy giggle.

ลูกหมาขี้เล่นทำให้แคธีหัวเราะคิกคัก

give *(กิฝ)* giving, gave

Mother gave Andy a bag.

แม่ให้กระเป๋าแก่แอนดี

give away *(กิฝ อะเว)*

Jimmy didn't want his pencils
so he gave them away.
จิมมีไม่ต้องการดินสอของเขา ดังนั้น
เขาจึงให้คนอื่นไป

give back *(กิฝ แบ็ค)*

The teacher is giving back the
exercise books.
ครูกำลังส่งสมุดแบบฝึกหัดคืน

give off *(กิฝ ออฟ)*

A fire gives off smoke.
ไฟทำให้เกิดควัน

give out *(กิฝ เอ๊าท)*

The headmaster is giving out
prizes to the best pupils.
ครูใหญ่กำลังมอบรางวัลให้นักเรียน
ที่ดีที่สุด

give up *(กิฝ อัฝ)*

> The robber gave himself up to the police.
>
> โจรยอมจำนนแก่ตำรวจ

glare *(กแล)* glaring, glared

> The two boys have stopped fighting but they are still glaring.
>
> เด็กสองคนนั้นเลิกชกต่อยกันแล้ว แต่พวกเขายังจ้องมองกันอยู่

glide *(กไลด)* gliding, glided

> A paper aeroplane glides through the air.
>
> เครื่องบินกระดาษร่อนขึ้นสู่อากาศ

glow *(กโล)* glowing, glowed

> The cat's eyes glow in the dark.
>
> ตาของแมวเรืองแสงในความมืด

glue *(กลู)* gluing, glued

Kathy glued a picture in the book.

แคธีติดภาพด้วยกาวในหนังสือ

go *(โก)* going, went

Andy goes for a drive in his toy car.

แอนดีไปขับรถเด็กเล่น

go away *(โก อะเว)*

"Go away, I want to be alone."

"ไปให้พ้น ผมต้องการอยู่คนเดียว"

go back *(โก แบ็ค)*

Linda forgot her umbrella. She went back home for it.

ลินดาลืมร่ม เธอจึงกลับบ้านเพื่อไปเอามัน

go on *(โก ออน)*

Mandy went on the roller

coaster.

แมนดีไปเล่นรถไฟเหาะตีลังกา

go out *(โก เอ๊าท)*

> Mr. and Mrs. Brown are going
> out to a party.
>
> นายและนางบราวน์กำลังออกไป
> งานเลี้ยง

go without *(โก วิธเอ๊าท)*

> Andy was naughty and had
> to go without dinner.
>
> แอนดีซุกซน จึงถูกอดอาหารเย็น

grab *(กแร็บ)* grabbing, grabbed

> The thief grabbed Aunt
> Molly's handbag.
>
> โจรคว้ากระเป๋าถือจากป้ามอลลี

greet *(กรีท)* greeting, greeted

> We greeted Grandmother with
> a bunch of flowers.

เราต้อนรับคุณยายด้วยช่อดอกไม้

grill *(กริล)* grilling, grilled

Father is grilling some sausages.

คุณพ่อกำลังย่างไส้กรอก

grin *(กริน)* grinning, grinned

Willy is grinning because his mother has given him a toy.

วิลลียิ้มเพราะว่าแม่ให้ของเล่นแก่เขา

grind *(ไกรนด)* grinding, ground

The cook is grinding nuts.

พ่อครัวกำลังบดถั่ว

grip *(กริพ)* gripping, gripped

Kathy gripped her mother's arm when they were on the ferris wheel.

แคธีจับแขนแม่แน่นตอนที่ทั้งสองอยู่บนชิงช้าสวรรค์

group *(กรูพ)* grouping, grouped

Simon grouped the toy ani-
mals into pets and wild ani-
mals.

ซิมมอนจัดกลุ่มของเล่นที่เป็นสัตว์
เป็นจำพวกสัตว์เลี้ยงและสัตว์ป่า

grow *(กโร)* growing, grew

Potatoes grow under the
ground.

หัวมันฝรั่งเจริญเติบโตใต้ดิน

growl *(กเราล)* growling, growled

The guard dog growled at the
stranger.

สุนัขเฝ้าบ้านคำรามใส่คนแปลกหน้า

grunt *(กรันท)* grunting, grunted

When pigs are hungry they
grunt.

เมื่อหมูหิวมันส่งเสียงออกทางจมูก

guard *(กาด)* guarding, guarded

The soldier guards the jewels from thieves.

ทหารปกป้องเพชรจากโจร

guess *(เก็ซ)* guessing, guessed

Close your eyes and guess what your presents are.

ปิดตาและทายว่าของขวัญคืออะไร

guide *(ไกด)* guiding, guided

The boy scout guide the blind man across the street.

ลูกเสือพาคนตาบอดข้ามถนน

gum *(กัม)* gumming, gummed

Linda gummed the two cards together to make a thicker card.

ลินดาใช้กาวติดกระดาษแข็งสองแผ่นเข้าด้วยกันเพื่อทำให้มันหนาขึ้น

gush *(กัฌ)* gushing, gushed

Look! The water is gushing out of the broken pipe.

ดูซิ! น้ำทะลักออกมาจากท่อแตก

H

hack *(แฮ็ค)* hacking, hacked

The fireman hacked the door with an axe.

พนักงานดับเพลิงพังประตูด้วยขวาน

hail *(เฮล)* hailing, hailed

Aunt Molly hailed a taxi to take her home.

ป้ามอลลีเรียกแท็กซี่เพื่อพาเธอกลับบ้าน

halt *(ฮอลท)* halting, halted

"Halt!" said the fireman. "You

cannot enter."

"หยุด" พนักงานดับเพลิงพูด "คุณเข้าไปไม่ได้"

halve *(ฮาฝ)* halving, halved

Mandy halved the orange before squeezing out the juice.

แมนดีตัดส้มเป็นสองซีกก่อนที่จะคั้นเป็นน้ำส้ม

hammer *(แฮม′เมอะ)* hammering, hammered

Jimmy hammered a nail into the wood.

จิมมีตอกตะปูเข้าไปในไม้

hand *(แฮ็นด)* handing, handed

The postman handed the letter to Kathy.

บุรุษไปรษณีย์ส่งจดหมายให้แคธี

hand out *(แฮ็นด เอ๊าท)*

Mother is handing out sweets

to the children.

คุณแม่กำลังส่งขนมหวานให้ลูก ๆ

handcuff *(แฮ็นด์´คัฟ)*

handcuffing, handcuffed

The policeman handcuffed the thief.

ตำรวจใส่กุญแจมือผู้ร้าย

handle *(แฮน´ดึล)* handling, handled

Linda handled the glasses with great care.

ลินดายกแก้วด้วยความระมัดระวัง

hang *(แฮ็ง)* hanging, hung

Andy hung his shirt up in the cupboard.

แอนดีแขวนเสื้อเชิ้ตของเขาไว้ในตู้

harm *(ฮาม)* harming, harmed

Is the big bad wolf going to harm Red Riding Hood?

เจ้าหมาป่าใจร้ายตัวนั้นกำลังจะทำ
ร้ายหนูน้อยหมวกแดงใช่ไหม

harvest *(ฮา'เฝ็ซท)* harvesting, harvested

The farmer is harvesting the crop.

ชาวนากำลังเก็บเกี่ยวผลผลิต

has *(แฮ็ส)* having, had

Jimmy has a blue cap.

จิมมีมีหมวกแก๊ปสีฟ้า

has got *(แฮ็ส ก็อท)*

Willy has got chicken pox.

วิลลีเป็นไข้อีสุกอีใส

has to *(แฮ็ส ทู)*

We have to drink water everyday.

เราต้องดื่มน้ำทุกวัน

hatch *(แฮ็ช)* hatching, hatched

The chicks hatched out of the

eggs.

ลูกไก่เจาะเปลือกไข่ออกมา

hate *(เฮท)* hating, hated

Willy hates to wake up early on cold mornings.

วิลลีไม่ชอบตื่นนอนในช่วงเช้าที่ อากาศหนาวเหน็บ

haul *(ฮอล)* hauling, hauled

The fishermen hauled their net onto the boat.

ชาวประมงลากแหเข้ามาที่เรือ

head *(เฮ็ด)* heading, headed

Jimmy headed the ball into the goal.

จิมมีโขกบอลเข้าไปตุงตาข่าย

The last time I saw Bobby, he was heading for home.

ครั้งสุดท้ายที่ฉันเห็นบ็อบบีเขากำลัง

เดินกลับบ้าน

heal *(ฮีล)* healing, healed

The cut on my arm has healed. I can take off the plaster.

แผลที่แขนของฉันหายดีแล้ว ฉันแกะพลาสเตอร์ปิดแผลออกได้

heap *(ฮีพ)* heaping, heaped

Kathy heaped her clothes on the floor.

แคธีกองเสื้อผ้าของเธอไว้บนพื้น

hear *(เฮีย)* hearing, heard

Mother heard the baby cry.

แม่ได้ยินเสียงลูกร้องไห้

heat *(ฮีท)* heating, heated

The fire heats the soup to boiling point.

ความร้อนจากไฟทำให้น้ำแกงเดือด

help *(เฮ็ลพ)* helping, helped

Kathy helps her mother make the bed.

แคธีช่วยแม่จัดเตียง

hiccup *(ฮีค´คัพ)* hiccuping, hiccuped

Poor Andy is hiccuping. How can he stop it?

แอนดีผู้น่าสงสารกำลังสะอึก   ทำ
อย่างไรเขาจึงจะหยุดสะอึกได้

hide *(ไฮด)* hiding, hid

The cat is hiding under a chair.

เจ้าแมวเหมียวหลบอยู่ใต้เก้าอี้

hike *(ไฮค)* hiking, hiked

We hiked round the lake the whole day.

เราใช้เวลาตลอดทั้งวันเดินเที่ยวไป
รอบ ๆ ทะเลสาบ

hire *(ไฮร)* hiring, hired

> The tourist hired a car for $50 a week.
>
> นักท่องเที่ยวเช่ารถในราคา 50 เหรียญ ต่อสัปดาห์

hiss *(ฮิซ)* hissing, hissed

> The snake hissed when Andy stepped on it.
>
> งูส่งเสียงขู่ฟ่อเพราะแอนดีไปเหยียบ มัน

hit *(ฮิท)* hitting, hit

> Willy hit the ball with the baseball bat.
>
> วิลลีตีลูกบอลด้วยไม้เบสบอล

hoist *(ฮอยซท)* hoisting, hoisted

> Look! Bobby is hoisting the school flag.
>
> ดูนี่ซิ! บ็อบบีกำลังชักธงขึ้นสู่ยอดเสา

hold *(ฮโลด)*   holding, held

> Andy is holding a baby orangutan's hand.
>
> แอนดีกำลังจูงมือเจ้าลิงอุรังอุตังตัวน้อย

hold on *(ฮโลด ออน)*

> Kathy held on tightly as her father carried her on his back.
>
> แคธีจับพ่อเอาไว้แน่น ขณะที่เธออยู่บนหลังของเขา

hold out *(ฮโลด เอ๊าท)*

> Willy held out his hand. He wanted to shake Mandy's hand.
>
> วิลลี่ยื่นมือของเขาออกมาเพื่อจับมือกับแมนดี

hold up *(ฮโลด อัพ)*

> Two masked men held up the

cashier and took all the money.

ชายสวมหน้ากากสองคนจับตัวแคช-
เชียร์ไว้ พร้อมขนเงินเอาไปจนหมด

honk *(ฮ็องค)* honking, honked

Geese honk at strangers.

ห่านส่งเสียงร้องใส่คนแปลกหน้า

hook *(ฮุค)* hooking, hooked

Jimmy has hooked a big fish.

จิมมีตกปลาตัวใหญ่ได้

hoot *(ฮูท)* hooting, hooted

Owls hoot at night.

นกเค้าแมวส่งเสียงร้องตอนกลางคืน

hop *(ฮ็อพ)* hopping, hopped

The children are hopping around the playground.

เด็ก ๆ กระโดดโลดเต้นรอบ ๆ สนาม
เด็กเล่น

hope *(โฮพ)*   hoping, hoped

Linda hoped the postman would bring a letter.

ลินดาหวังว่าบุรุษไปรษณีย์จะนำจด-หมายมาให้เธอ

hose *(โฮส)*   hosing, hosed

Father is hosing the car down.

คุณพ่อเปิดสายยางล้างรถ

howl *(เฮาล)*   howling, howled

The baby howled when it fell out of its cot.

เด็กทารกส่งเสียงร้องด้วยความเจ็บเมื่อตกจากเปล

huddle *(ฮัด′ดึล)*   huddling, huddled

The chicks are huddling together to keep warm.

ลูกเจี๊ยบเบียดตัวกันเป็นกลุ่มเพื่อให้เกิดความอุ่น

huff *(ฮัฟ)* huffing, huffed

The children huffed and puffed after the run.

เด็ก ๆ แสดงอาการเหนื่อยหอบหลัง เสร็จจากการวิ่ง

hug *(ฮัก)* hugging, hugged

Mother hugs me when I come home from school.

แม่กอดฉันเมื่อฉันกลับจากโรงเรียน มาถึงบ้าน

hum *(ฮัม)* humming, hummed

Willy is humming as he walks to the park.

วิลลีฮัมเพลงขณะที่เขาเดินไปสวน สาธารณะ

hunt *(ฮันท)* hunting, hunted

Grandmother is hunting for her glasses.

คุณย่ากำลังหาแว่นตาของท่าน

hurl *(เฮิล)* hurling, hurled

Jimmy hurled the ball as far as he could.

จิมมีปาลูกบอลไปให้ไกลที่สุดเท่าที่จะไกลได้

hurry *(เฮอ′ริ)* hurrying, hurried

Jimmy got up late and hurries to get dressed.

จิมมีตื่นสายและต้องรีบแต่งตัวให้ทัน

hurry up *(เฮอ′ริ อัพ)*

Hurry up! If you want to get to school on time.

เร็วๆ เข้า จะได้ไปโรงเรียนให้ทันเวลา

hurt *(เฮิท)* hurting, hurt

Peter hurt his toe on a rock.

ปีเตอร์เดินเตะก้อนหินและเจ็บที่หัวแม่เท้า

hush *(ฮัฌ)* hushing, hushed

> Hush! Don't wake the baby.
>
> เงียบหน่อย! เดี๋ยวเด็กจะตื่น

I

---

imagine *(อิแมจ' อิน)* imagining, imagined

> Kathy imagined she was a movie star.
>
> แคธีวาดภาพว่าตัวเองเป็นดารา ภาพยนตร์

imitate *(อิม'อิเทท)* imitating, imitated

> Willy can imitate Superman very well.
>
> วิลลีแต่งตัวเลียนแบบซูเปอร์แมน เหมือนจริงมาก

increase *(อิน'ครีซ)* increasing, increased

> If you blow more air into the

balloon, its size will increase.

ถ้าเป่าลมเพิ่มเข้าไป ลูกโป่งจะโตขึ้น

inform *(อินฟอม′)* informing, informed

The teacher informed the children where to go to fly their
kites.

คุณครูบอกนักเรียนว่าจะไปเล่นว่าว
ได้ที่ไหน

injure *(อิน′เจอะ)* injuring, injured

Simon fell down and injured
his arm.

ซิมมอนตกจากที่สูงและเจ็บที่แขน

inspect *(อินซเพคท′)* inspecting, inspected

Bobby dropped his kite. He
inspected it to make sure that
it was all right.

บ็อบบีดึงว่าวลงมาตรวจดู   เพื่อให้
มั่นใจว่าทุกอย่างไม่มีปัญหา

install *(อินซทอล′)* installing, installed

The workers are installing a new pole.

คนงานก่อเสาต้นใหม่

instruct *(อินซทรัคท′)* instructing, instructed

The teacher is instructing the children how to fly a kite.

คุณครูกำลังสอนวิธีเล่นว่าวให้นัก–เรียน

interrupt *(อินเทะรัพท′)*

interrupting, interrupted

Andy interrupted his teacher who was talking.

แอนดีพูดแทรกขึ้นมาในขณะที่ครูกำลังพูด

interview *(อิน′เทิฝยู)*

interviewing, interviewed

The reporter interviewed

Bobby. He asked him about the party.

นักข่าวสัมภาษณ์บ็อบบีเกี่ยวกับงาน ปาร์ตี้

introduce *(อินทโระดยูซ´)*

introducing, introduced

Mandy introduced Terry to Jimmy.

แมนดีแนะนำเทอร์รี่ให้จิมมีรู้จัก

invent *(อินเฝนท´)* inventing, invented

The scientist invented a machine to walk a dog.

นักวิทยาศาสตร์ประดิษฐ์เครื่องมือจูง สุนัข (ไปเดินเล่น)

invite *(อินไฝท´)* inviting, invited

Bobby was invited to a fancy-dress party.

บ็อบบีได้รับเชิญไปร่วมงานแฟนซี

ปาร์ตี้

iron *(ไอ'เอิน)* ironing, ironed

Father is ironing his shirt.

พ่อกำลังรีดเสื้อเชิ้ตของเขา

itch *(อิช)* itching, itched

Peter's arm itches because a mosquito bit him there.

ปีเตอร์คันที่แขนเพราะถูกยุงกัด

J

jack up *(แจ็ค อัพ)*

Father jacked up the car to change the tire.

พ่อใช้แม่แรงยกรถเพื่อเปลี่ยนยาง

jam *(แจ็ม)* jamming, jammed

Andy jammed the clothes in the suitcase.

แอนดียัดเสื้อผ้าเข้ากระเป๋า

jerk *(เจิค)* jerking, jerked

The car jerked a few times and then stopped suddenly.

รถกระตุกอยู่สองสามครั้งก่อนเครื่องจะดับ

jingle *(จิง'กึล)* jingling, jingled

There are bells on the dog's collar. They jingle when it moves.

กระดิ่งที่ปลอกคอสุนัขจะส่งเสียงกรุ๊งกริ๊งขึ้นเวลาที่มันขยับตัว

jog *(จ็อก)* jogging, jogged

Bobby jogged around the track.

บ็อบบีวิ่งเหยาะ ๆ ไปตามลู่วิ่ง

join *(จอยน)* joining, joined

Willy can join two pieces

string with a knot.

วิลลีสามารถผูกปมต่อเชือกสองเส้น
เข้าด้วยกัน

joke *(โจค)* joking, joked

The children are joking with
one another. They are telling
funny stories.

พวกเด็ก ๆ กำลังหัวเราะสนุกกันใหญ่
พวกเขาผลัดกันเล่าเรื่องตลกขบขัน

jot *(จ็อท)* jotting, jotted

Peter jotted down my phone
number on a piece of paper.

ปีเตอร์จดเบอร์โทรศัพท์ของฉันลง
บนแผ่นกระดาษ

judge *(จัจ)* judging, judged

Kathy's dog was judged the
best dog in the show.

สุนัขของแคธีได้รับการตัดสินให้เป็น

สุนัขที่ดีที่สุดในงานประกวด

jumble *(จั่ม'บึล)* jumbling, jumbled

The naughty girl jumbled her
clothes up.

เด็กผู้หญิงซุกซนคนนี้ทำเสื้อผ้าปะ
ปนยุ่งเหยิงไปหมด

jump *(จัมพ)* jumping, jumped

The cat jumped over the
sleeping dog and ran off as
quickly as it could.

แมวกระโดดข้ามสุนัขที่กำลังนอน
หลับ และวิ่งหนีไปอย่างเร็วที่สุด

jump at *(จัมพ แอ็ท)*

The dog jumped at the man
passing by.

เจ้าสุนัขตัวนี้กระโดดเข้าหาผู้ชายที่
กำลังเดินผ่านไป

jump to *(จัมพ ทู)*

> The dogs jumped to attention
> when the judge arrived.
> บรรดาสุนัขพากันยืดตัวตรง   เมื่อผู้
> ตัดสินเดินเข้ามา

jump up *(จัมพ อัพ)*

> Puss jumped up on to Andy's
> lap.
> แมวเหมียวกระโดดขึ้นมาบนตักของ
> แอนดี

K

keep *(คีพ)* keeping, kept

> Helen keeps her pet snake in
> a basket.
> เฮเลนเลี้ยงงูของเธอในตะกร้า

keep away *(คีพ อะเว)*

> Keep away from the dog. It bites!
>
> อย่าเข้าใกล้สุนัข มันกัด!

keep off *(คีพ ออฟ)*

> Keep off the grass. There are prickles.
>
> อย่าเข้าไปเหยียบต้นหญ้า   มันมีหนาม

keep up *(คีพ อัพ)*

> Bobby can run faster than Willy. Willy can't keep up with him.
>
> บ็อบบีวิ่งเร็วกว่าวิลลี   จนวิลลีตามไม่ทัน

kick *(คิค)* kicking, kicked

> Terry kicked the ball over the fence.

เทอร์รีเตะบอลข้ามรั้วออกไป

kill *(คิล)* killing, killed

> The prince became a hero when he killed a dragon.
>
> เจ้าชายกลายเป็นวีรบุรุษ เมื่อสามารถปราบมังกรร้ายได้สำเร็จ

kiss *(คิซ)* kissing, kissed

> Mother kissed Kathy on her cheek.
>
> แม่จูบแคธีที่แก้ม

kneel *(นีล)* kneeling, kneeled

> Jimmy kneels down to pray.
>
> จิมมีคุกเข่าลงเพื่อสวดมนต์

knit *(นิท)* knitting, knitted

> Grandmother is knitting a jumper.
>
> คุณย่ากำลังถักเสื้อไหมพรม

knock *(น็อค)* knocking, knocked

> The postman is knocking on the door. He has a parcel to deliver.
>
> บุรุษไปรษณีย์เคาะประตูเพื่อจะส่งพัสดุ

knot *(น็อท)* knotting, knotted

> Mandy is knotting a scarf round her neck.
>
> แมนดีผูกผ้าพันคอรอบคอของเธอ

know *(โน)* knowing, knew

> Peter knows the answer to the sum.
>
> ปีเตอร์รู้คำตอบของเลขข้อนี้

L

ladle (เล'ดึล) ladling, ladled

The old woman is ladling out soup to the children.

หญิงชราคนนี้กำลังตักซุปแจกให้เด็กๆ

land (แล็นด) landing, landed

Bobby's ball landed in Aunt Molly's soup.

ลูกบอลของบ็อบบีตกลงไปในถ้วยซุปของคุณป้ามอลลี

last (ลาชท) lasting, lasted

I wonder how long the rain will last.

ฉันสงสัยว่าฝนจะตกอีกนานสักเท่าไร

laugh (ลาฟ) laughing, laughed

Andy is laughing because

Jane is tickling him.

แอนดีหัวเราะเพราะถูกเจนจี้เส้น

laugh at *(ลาฟ แอ็ท)*

The children are laughing at the clown's tricks.

เด็ก ๆ กำลังหัวเราะกับลูกเล่นชั้นเชิง ของตัวตลก

lay *(เล)* laying, laid

Kathy is laying the table for dinner.

แคธีกำลังจัดโต๊ะสำหรับอาหารเย็น

Our hen lays two eggs every day.

แม่ไก่ของเราออกไข่ 2 ฟองทุก ๆ วัน

lead *(ลีด)* leading, leaded

Andy is leading his dog up the windy path.

แอนดีจูงสุนัขขึ้นไปตามทางที่มีลมแรง

lead up *(ลีด อัพ)*

> The winding path leads up to the haunted house.
>
> ทางคดเคี้ยวนี้นำไปสู่บ้านผีสิง

leak *(ลีค)* leaking, leaked

> The roof is leaking.
>
> หลังคารั่ว

lean *(ลีน)* leaning, leaned or leant

> The ladder leans against the wall.
>
> บันไดพาดกับกำแพง

leap *(ลีพ)* leaping, leapt

> Helen opened the box and a frog leapt out.
>
> เฮเลนเปิดกล่อง กบตัวหนึ่งกระโดดออกมา

learn *(เลิน)* learning, learned, or learnt

> Jane is learning how to play

the piano.

เจนกำลังหัดเล่นเปียโน

leave *(ลีฝ)* leaving, left

Willy left his school bag at
bus stop.

วิลลีวางกระเป๋านักเรียนของเขาทิ้งไว้
ที่ป้ายรถเมล์

leave out   *(ลีฝ เอ๊าท)*

The boys were playing mar-
bles and Linda was left out.

พวกเด็กผู้ชายกำลังเล่นลูกหินกัน
ปล่อยให้ลินดาอยู่คนเดียว

lend *(เล็นด)* lending, lent

Mandy lent Linda her music
book.

แมนดีให้ลินดายืมหนังสือดนตรีของ
เธอ

let *(เล็ท)* letting, let

>The teacher let Andy play the guitar.
>
>คุณครูปล่อยให้แอนดีเล่นกีตาร์

let down *(เล็ท ดาวน)*

>Rapunzel let down her long hair.
>
>ราพันเซลสยายผมยาวของเธอลงมา

let go *(เล็ท โก)*

>Bobby let go of the balloon and it floated away.
>
>บ็อบบีปล่อยลูกโป่งและมันลอยขึ้นไป

let in *(เล็ท อิน)*

>Open the door and let in Simon.
>
>เปิดประตูให้ซิมมอนเข้ามา

let out *(เล็ท เอ๊าท)*

>Willy let out a cry of pain

when he hit his finger.

วิลลีร้องด้วยความเจ็บปวด เมื่อเขา
ตีถูกนิ้วตัวเอง

lick *(ลิค)* licking, licked

Andy is licking a lollipop.

แอนดีกำลังเลียอมยิ้ม

lie *(ไล)* lying, lied

Andy is lying.

แอนดีกำลังโกหก

The cat is lying in the washing basket.

แมวเหมียวกำลังนอนในตะกร้าซัก
เสื้อผ้า

  lie down   *(ไล ดาวน)*

Grandmother is tired. She is
lying down on the sofa.

คุณย่ารู้สึกเหนื่อย ท่านจึงนอนพัก
บนโซฟา

lift *(ลิฟท)* lifting, lifted

Willy lifted Jimmy up.

วิลลีจับจิมมียกขึ้น

light *(ไลท)* lighting, lighted

Grandfather is very careful when he lights the candle.

คุณปู่ระมัดระวังมากเวลาที่จุดเทียน

like *(ไลค)* liking, liked

Jimmy likes the trumpet. Kathy likes the flute.

จิมมีชอบทรัมเป็ต แคธีชอบฟลุต

limp *(ลิมพ)* limping, limped

The dog has a sore paw and is limping.

สุนัขเจ็บที่อุ้งเท้าและเดินโขยกเขยก

line *(ไลน)* lining, lined

Kathy is lining the shelf with paper.

แคธีปูชั้นวางหนังสือด้วยกระดาษ

line up *(ไลน อัพ)*

> Mandy lined up the chair for the concert.
>
> แมนดีจัดเก้าอี้สำหรับผู้ชมคอนเสิร์ต

link *(ลิงค)* linking, linked

> The new road links the two towns.
>
> ถนนสายใหม่เชื่อมต่อสองเมืองเข้าด้วยกัน

list *(ลิซท)* listing, listed

> Aunt Molly is listing the things she needs to buy.
>
> คุณป้ามอลลีกำลังเขียนรายการของที่เธอจะต้องซื้อ

listen *(ลีซึน)* listening, listened

> Andy is listening to the radio.
>
> แอนดีกำลังฟังวิทยุ

litter *(ลีท'เทอะ)* littering, littered

Andy has littered the floor with sweet wrappers.

แอนดีทิ้งกระดาษห่อลูกอมกระจัด กระจายไปตามพื้นห้อง

live *(ลิฝ)* living, lived

There was an old woman who lived in a shoe.

มีหญิงชราคนหนึ่ง ผู้ซึ่งอาศัยอยู่ใน รองเท้า

live on *(ลิฝ ออน)*

Monkeys live on fruit and nuts.

ลิงกินผลไม้และถั่วเป็นอาหาร

load *(โลด)* loading, loaded

The men are loading the van with sacks of flour.

พวกผู้ชายกำลังยกกระสอบแป้งขึ้น

ไปไว้บนรถบรรทุก

lock *(ล็อค)* locking, locked

> Every night father locks the door.
>
> คุณพ่อล็อคประตูทุก ๆ คืน

> **lock up** *(ล็อค อัพ)*
>
> > Aunt Molly locks up her jewels in a safe.
> >
> > คุณป้ามอลลีเก็บเครื่องเพชรพลอย เข้าตู้เซฟ

loll *(ล็อล)* lolling, lolled

> Willy is lolling on the sofa, doing nothing.
>
> วิลลีนอนเอกเขนกอยู่บนโซฟาไม่ทำ อะไร

long *(ล็อง)* longing, longed

> Andy is longing for chocolate. It's his favorite food.

แอนดียอยากกินช็อกโกแลตของโปรด
ของเขา

look *(ลุค)* looking, looked

Look at the aeroplane flying
upside down.

ดูที่เครื่องบินนั่นซิ มันบินหงายท้อง

look after *(ลุค อาฟเทอะ)*

Mother looks after the baby
all day.

คุณแม่ดูแลลูกที่ยังแบเบาะตลอดวัน

look for *(ลุค ฟอร)*

The children are looking for
the lost ball.

เด็ก ๆ กำลังหาลูกบอลที่หายไป

look out *(ลุค เอ๊าท)*

Look out! A branch is falling
down.

ระวัง! กิ่งไม้กำลังตกลงมา

look up *(ลุค อัพ)*

> Helen doesn't know how to spell a word. She is looking it up in the dictionary.
>
> เฮเลนไม่รู้วิธีสะกดคำ เธอกำลังค้นหาในพจนานุกรม

loop *(ลูพ)* looping, looped

> The cowboy loops the rope round the bull.
>
> หนุ่มคาวบอยใช้เชือกคล้องวัวกระทิง

lose *(ลูส)* losing, lost

> Jimmy dropped $10 and lost it.
>
> จิมมีทำธนบัตร 10 ดอลลาร์ตกและหายไป

love *(ลัฝ)* loving, loved

> I love my grandmother.
>
> ฉันรักคุณย่าของฉัน

lunch *(ลันช)* lunching, lunched

Andy is lunching with his aunt.

แอนดีกำลังทานอาหารเที่ยงกับคุณ
ป้าของเขา

M

mail *(เมล)* mailing, mailed

Kathy has written a letter to her friend. She is mailing it.

แคธีเขียนจดหมายไปหาเพื่อน เธอ
ส่งไปทางไปรษณีย์

make *(เมค)* making, made

Willy is making a sandwich for himself.

วิลลีทำแซนวิชให้ตัวเอง

make for *(เมค ฟอร)*

> Jimmy made for the door when Linda ran after him with a rolling pin.
>
> จิมมีวิ่งหนีไปทางประตู เมื่อลินดาถือไม้นวดแป้งไล่ตี

make from *(เมค ฟร็อม)*

> This jam is made from strawberries.
>
> แยมนี้ทำมาจากสตรอเบอร์รี่

make of *(เมค ออฝ)*

> This jar is made of glass.
>
> เหยือกใบนี้ทำมาจากแก้ว

make off *(เมค ออฟ)*

> The thief made off with a big cake.
>
> โจรขโมยเค้กก้อนโตไป

make out *(เมค เอ๊าท)*

> The stranger wore a mask and Helen couldn't make out who he was.
>
> คนแปลกหน้าสวมหน้ากาก ทำให้เฮเลนไม่รู้ว่าเขาเป็นใคร

march *(มาช)* marching, marched

> The band marched down the street playing music.
>
> วงโยธวาทิตเดินแถวบรรเลงไปตามถนน

mark *(มาค)* marking, marked

> The teacher is marking the exercise books.
>
> คุณครูกำลังตรวจแบบฝึกหัด

marry *(แม'ริ)* marrying, married

> Aunt Jane married a soldier.
>
> คุณป้าเจนแต่งงานกับทหาร

mash *(แม็ฌ)* mashing, mashed

Jimmy is mashing the pota
toes.

จิมมีกำลังบดมันฝรั่ง

mask *(มาซค)* masking, masked

The children mask their faces
for the party.

พวกเด็ก ๆ สวมหน้ากากไปร่วมงาน
ปาร์ตี้

match *(แม็ช)* matching, matched

Jimmy's socks do not match.

ถุงเท้าของจิมมีไม่เข้าคู่กัน

measure *(เมฉ′เออะ)* measuring, measured

Andy is measuring the flour
with a cup.

แอนดีกำลังตวงแป้งด้วยถ้วยตวง

meet *(มีท)* meeting, met

Bobby met Mandy outside the

post office.

บ็อบบีพบแมนดีด้านนอกของที่ทำ
การไปรษณีย์

melt *(เม็ลท)* melting, melted

Ice melts when you take it
out of the freezer.

น้ำแข็งละลายเมื่อคุณเอามันออก
จากช่องแข็ง

mend *(เม็นด)* mending, mended

Bobby is mending the broken
toaster.

บ็อบบีกำลังซ่อมเครื่องปิ้งขนมปัง

mess up *(เมส อัพ)*

The wind messed up Kathy's
hair.

ลมทำให้ผมของแคธียุ่งไปหมด

mew *(มยู)* mewing, mewed

The cat is mewing. It wants

food.

แมวส่งเสียงร้องเหมียว ๆ มันต้องการ
อาหาร

milk *(มิลค)*   milking, milked

The farmer is milking the
cow.

เกษตรกรกำลังรีดนมวัว

mime *(ไมม)*   miming, mimed

Andy is miming that he
wants a drink.

แอนดีใช้ภาษามือบอกใบ้ว่าเขาต้อง
การเครื่องดื่ม

mince *(มินซ)*   mincing, minced

Simon is mincing the meat to
make pies.

ซิมอนกำลังบดเนื้อเพื่อทำพาย

mine *(ไมน)*   mining, mined

The miners are mining coal

from under the ground.

คนงานเหมืองแร่กำลังขุดถ่านหิน
จากใต้ดิน

miss *(มิซ)* missing, missed

The paper airplane just missed
Linda's head.

เครื่องบินกระดาษเฉี่ยวหัวลินดาไป
นิดเดียว

miss out *(มิซ เอ๊าท)*

When the teacher was giving
the children crayons, he missed
out Willy.

ตอนคุณครูแจกดินสอสีให้นักเรียน
คุณครูลืมแจกให้วิลลี

mistake *(มิซเทค′)* mistaking, mistook

Andy mistook pepper for salt.

แอนดีเข้าใจผิดคิดว่าขวดพริกไทย
เป็นขวดเกลือ

mix *(มิคซ)* mixing, mixed

> Willy mixed flour and water
> to make a dough.
> วิลลีผสมผงแป้งกับน้ำเข้าด้วยกัน
> เพื่อทำแป้งขนมปัง

model *(มอ'ดึล)* modelling, modelled

> Kathy is modelling a party
> dress.
> แคธีเดินแบบชุดงานปาร์ตี้

moo *(มู)* mooing, mooed

> Cows moo.
> วัวส่งเสียงร้องมอ ๆ

mount *(เมานท)* mounting, mounted

> Bobby is mounting his bicycle.
> บ็อบบีขึ้นขี่จักรยาน

move *(มูฝ)* moving, moved

> Jimmy picked up his books
> and moved them to another

desk.

จิมมีหยิบหนังสือแล้วนำไปวางไว้ที่
โต๊ะอีกตัวหนึ่ง

move in *(มูฝ อิน)*

Mr. and Mrs. Sharp are moving in next door.

คุณชาร์ปและภรรยาย้ายมาอาศัยอยู่
บ้านข้าง ๆ

move out *(มูฝ เอ๊าท)*

Bobby is moving out of the
haunted house.

บ็อบบีขนของย้ายออกจากบ้านผีสิง

mow *(โม)*   mowing, mowed

Father is mowing the lawn.

คุณพ่อกำลังตัดหญ้าในสนาม

N

nail *(เนล)* nailing, nailed

> The workman is nailing a sign on the fence.
>
> คนงานกำลังตอกตะปูติดป้ายบนรั้ว

name *(เนม)* naming, named

> The baby was named Melissa Anne.
>
> เด็กคนนี้ถูกตั้งชื่อว่า เมลิสซา แอน

nap *(แน็พ)* napping, napped

> Willy is napping in the garden.
>
> วิลลีกำลังม่อยหลับอยู่ในสวน

need *(นีด)* needing, needed

> The workman needs a new pair of shoes.
>
> คนงานคนนี้จำเป็นจะต้องมีรองเท้า

คู่ใหม่ / คนงานคนนี้ต้องการรองเท้า
คู่ใหม่

neigh *(เน)* neighing, neighed

Horses neigh.

ม้าส่งเสียงร้องฮี้ ๆ

net *(เน็ท)* netting, netted

Jimmy has netted a big fish.

จิมมีจับปลาตัวใหญ่ได้ด้วยการใช้สวิง

nibble *(นีบึล)* nibbling, nibbled

The mouse is nibbling at the
bread.

หนูกำลังแทะขนมปัง

nip *(นิพ)* nipping, nipped

The dog is nipping the man
on the leg.

สุนัขกำลังงับขาชายคนนี้

nod *(น็อด)* nodding, nodded

> Uncle Roy is nodding his head to show that he wants the coffee.
>
> คุณลุงรอยพยักหน้าว่าเขาต้องการกาแฟ

notice *(โน'ทิซ)* noticing, noticed

> Mr. Trump noticed a man sneaking out through the back gate.
>
> คุณทรัมป์สังเกตเห็นชายคนหนึ่งเล็ดลอดออกไปทางประตูหลัง

nudge *(นัจ)* nudging, nudged

> Uncle Roy is nudging a workman who has fallen asleep.
>
> คุณลุงรอยใช้ข้อศอกถองคนงานที่กำลังเผลอหลับ

nurse *(เนิซ)* nursing, nursed

> Mother nursed Andy when he had measles.
>
> คุณแม่ดูแลแอนดีตอนที่เขาป่วยเป็นโรคหัด

O

obey *(โอะเบ′)* obeying, obeyed

> Mother said, "Go to bed" and I had to obey.
>
> คุณแม่ออกคำสั่ง "ไปนอนเดี๋ยวนี้" ฉันจึงต้องปฏิบัติตาม

occupy *(ออค′คิวไพ)* occupying, occupied

> Peter wanted to use the bathroom but it was occupied.
>
> ปีเตอร์ต้องการใช้ห้องน้ำ แต่ห้องน้ำไม่ว่าง

offer *(ออฟเฟอะ)* offering, offered

> Bobby offered to help Helen repair her bicycle.
>
> บ็อบบีเสนอตัวช่วยเฮเลนซ่อมจักร-
> ยาน

oil *(ออยล)* oiling, oiled

> Bobby oiled the wheels of his toy car.
>
> บ็อบบีหยอดน้ำมันที่ล้อรถเด็กเล่น
> ของเขา

open *(โอเพ็น)* opening, opened

> Linda is opening her birth-day presents.
>
> ลินดากำลังแกะกล่องของขวัญวัน
> เกิดของเธอ

operate *(ออพเออะเรท)* operating, operated

> The surgeon is operating on a man who has broken his leg.

แพทย์กำลังผ่าตัดชายที่ขาหัก

order *(ออ'เดอะ)* ordering, ordered

> Kathy ordered a hamburger and French-fried for lunch.
>
> แคธีสั่งแฮมเบอร์เกอร์และเฟรนช์–ฟรายสำหรับมื้อเที่ยง

overtake *(โอเฝอะเทค')* overtaking, overtook

> Our car is overtaking the truck.
>
> รถเก๋งของเราแซงหน้ารถบรรทุก

overturn *(โอเฝอะเทิน')*

overturning, overturned

> The boat overturned in the storm.
>
> เรือถูกพายุพัดจนพลิกคว่ำ

owe *(โอ)* owing, owed

> Peter borrows $1 from Jimmy.
> He owes Jimmy $1.

ปีเตอร์ยืมเงิน 1 เหรียญจากจิมมี เขา
ค้างจิมมีอยู่ 1 เหรียญ

own *(โอน)* owning, owned

Mandy saved up her money
and now owns a new bicycle.
แมนดีเก็บออมเงินจนกระทั่งได้เป็น
เจ้าของจักรยานคันใหม่

P

pack *(แพ็ค)* packing, packed

Kathy is packing food for a
picnic.
แคธีจัดเตรียมอาหารใส่กระเป๋า
สำหรับปิกนิก

pack up *(แพ็ค อัพ)*

The picnic is over. The children are packing up the things.

ปิกนิกเลิกแล้ว เด็กๆ เก็บข้าวเก็บ
ของกลับ

paddle *(แพ่ ดดีล)* paddling, paddled

Bobby is paddling the canoe
down the river.

บ็อบบีพายเรือแคนูไปตามแม่น้ำ

paint *(เพนท่)* painting, painted

Andy is painting a picture of
his family.

แอนดีวาดรูปครอบครัวของเขา

pair *(แพ)* pairing, paired

The socks are all mixed up.
Can you pair them again?

ถุงเท้าผสมปนเปกันหมด คุณจัดเป็น
คู่ๆ อีกครั้งได้ไหม?

pant *(แพ็นท)* panting, panted

The dog is panting after running up the steep slope.

สุนัขกำลังหอบหลังจากวิ่งขึ้นเนินชัน

parachute *(แพ´ระฌูท)*

   parachuting, parachuted

        Linda is parachuting into the forest.

        ลินดาโดดร่มลงในป่า

park *(พาค)* parking, parked

        Mother parked the car next to a van.

        คุณแม่จอดรถยนต์ข้าง ๆ รถตู้

part *(พาท)* parting, parted

        Terry always parts his hair on the left.

        เทอรี่แสกผมทางซ้ายเสมอ

pass *(พาซ)* passing, passed

        Jimmy is passing the salt to Linda.

        จิมมี่ส่งเกลือให้ลินดา

paste *(เพซท)* pasting, pasted

>Bobby is pasting a poster on the walk.
>
>บ็อบบีกำลังติดโปสเตอร์ข้างทางเท้า

pat *(แพ็ท)* patting, patted

>Linda is patting the dog on the head.
>
>ลินดากำลังลูบหัวสุนัข

patch *(แพ็ซ)* patching, patched

>Mother is patching a hole in the knee of Andy's jeans.
>
>คุณแม่กำลังปะกางเกงยีนส์ของแอน–ดีที่บริเวณเข่า

patrol *(พัทโรล′)* patrolling, patrolled

>Two policemen are patrolling our street.
>
>ตำรวจสองคนกำลังตรวจตราถนนของเรา

pave *(เพฝ)* paving, paved

> The workmen are paving thc
> road.
>
> คนงานกำลังปูถนน

paw *(พอ)* pawing, pawed

> The dog is pawing the rubber
> bone.
>
> สุนัขกำลังตะกุยกระดูกยาง

pay *(เพ)* paying, paid

> Father is paying for the gro-
> ceries at the check-out counter.
>
> คุณพ่อกำลังจ่ายเงินค่าของชำที่
> เคาน์เตอร์เก็บเงิน

pay back *(เพ แบ็ค)*

> Jimmy is paying back the ten
> dollars Peter lent him.
>
> จิมมีใช้คืนเงินสิบดอลลาร์ที่เขายืมมา
> จากปีเตอร์

peck *(เพ็ค)* pecking, pecked

The little bird is pecking at the apple.

เจ้านกน้อยกำลังจิกผลแอปเปิ้ล

pedal *(เพด´ แอ็ล)* pedalling, pedalled

Bobby is pedalling his new bicycle up the hill.

บ็อบบีปั่นจักรยานคันใหม่ของเขา ขึ้นเขา

peel *(พีล)* peeling, peeled

Linda is peeling the orange.

ลินดากำลังปอกเปลือกส้ม

peep *(พีพ)* peeping, peeped

Mandy is peeping through the window.

แมนดีแอบมองผ่านทางหน้าต่าง

peg *(เพ็ก)* pegging, pegged

Mother is pegging her washing.

แม่กำลังใช้ตัวหนีบหนีบเสื้อที่ตากไว้
กับราว

perch *(เพิช)* perching, perched

The bird has perched on a
branch.

นกตัวนี้กำลังเกาะอยู่ที่กิ่งไม้

perform *(เพอะฟอม′)* performing, performed

The magician is performing a
trick.

นักมายากลกำลังเล่นกล

photograph *(โฟโทะกราฟ)*

photographing, photographed

Jimmy is photographing the
playful kitten.

จิมมีกำลังถ่ายรูปลูกแมวขี้เล่น

pick *(พิค)* picking, picked

Jimmy is picking mangoes
from a tree in his garden.

จิมมีกำลังปลิดผลมะม่วงจากต้นใน
สวนของเขา

pick out *(ฟิค เอ๊าท)*

Mandy has picked out all the
black jelly beans.
แมนดีคัดเม็ดขนมเยลลีสีดำออก

pick up *(พิค อัพ)*

Willy is picking up the pieces
of broken glass.
วิลลีกำลังเก็บเศษแก้วที่แตกกระจาย

picnic *(พีค' นิค)* picnicking, picked

The children are picnicking
by the river.
เด็ก ๆ กำลังปิกนิกอยู่ริมแม่น้ำ

pierce *(เพียซ)* piercing, pierced

The arrow pierced the apple.
ลูกธนูเสียบเข้าที่ผลแอปเปิ้ล

pile *(ไพล)* piling, piled

> Jane is piling up the sand to
> make a sandcastle.
>
> เจนกำลังก่อกองทรายเพื่อทำเป็น
> ปราสาททราย

pin *(พิน)* pinning, pinned

> Our teacher pinned a notice
> on the noticeboard.
>
> ครูของเราใช้หมุดติดป้ายประกาศที่
> กระดาน

pinch *(พินซ)* pinching, pinched

> A monster sneaked up and
> pinched my arm.
>
> สัตว์ประหลาดย่องเข้ามาและหยิกที่
> แขนของฉัน

place *(พเลซ)* placing, placed

> Mother placed the antique
> vase on the mantelpiece.

คุณแม่วางแจกันโบราณไว้เหนือ
เตาผิง

plant *(พลานท)* planting, planted

Mother is planting some
daisy seeds in the garden.

คุณแม่กำลังเพาะเมล็ดพันธุ์ต้นเดซี่
ในสวน

play *(เพล)* playing, played

Mandy and Kathy are playing
hopscotch in the playground.

แมนดีและแคธีเล่นต้องเตในสนาม
เด็กเล่น

plough *(เพลา)* ploughing, ploughed

The farmer ploughs his field
before planting corn.

ชาวไร่พรวนดินก่อนจะปลูกข้าวโพด

pluck *(พลัค)* plucking, plucked

Jimmy is busy plucking

apples.

จิมมีกำลังยุ่งอยู่กับการเก็บผลแอป
เปิ้ล

point *(พอยนท)* pointing, pointed

Andy is pointing a finger at
the puppies that chewed his
father's slippers.

แอนดีชี้นิ้วไปที่ลูกสุนัขซึ่งกัดรองเท้า
แตะของพ่อของเขา

  point out *(พอยนท เอ๊าท)*

The guide points out the old
tower to the tourists.

มัคคุเทศก์ชี้ให้นักท่องเที่ยวดูหอเก่า
แก่

poke *(โพค)* poking, poked

Andy is poking a stick into
the sand.

แอนดีปักไม้บนพื้นทราย

polish *(พอล' อิฌ)* polishing, polished

Father has washed the car. He is now polishing it.

พ่อพึ่งล้างรถเสร็จ ตอนนี้ท่านกำลังขัดรถให้เป็นเงา

pose *(โพส)* posing, posed

Andy is posing for a photograph.

แอนดียืนโพสท่าให้ถ่ายรูป

post *(โพซท)* posting, posted

Kathy posted a letter to her French penpal.

แคธีส่งจดหมายให้เพื่อนชาวฝรั่งเศสที่ติดต่อกันทางจดหมาย

pounce *(เพานซ)* pouncing, pounced

The cat pounced on the mouse.

เจ้าแมวกระโดดตะครุบหนู

pound *(เพานด)* pounding, pounded

> Mother is pounding the meat
> to make it tender.
>
> คุณแม่กำลังทุบชิ้นเนื้อให้นุ่ม

pour *(โพ)* pouring, poured

> Aunt Molly is pouring the tea
> into the cups.
>
> ป้ามอลลีกำลังเทน้ำชาใส่ถ้วย

pour on *(โพ ออน)*

> Jimmy poured water on the
> fire to put it out.
>
> จิมมีเอาน้ำราดเพื่อจะดับไฟ

powder *(เพา′เดอะ)* powdering, powdered

> Aunt Molly is powdering her
> face.
>
> ป้ามอลลีกำลังทาแป้งที่หน้า

practise *(พแรค′ทิซ)* practising, practised

> Kathy practises hard for a

ballet performance.

แคธีซ้อมหนักก่อนการแสดงบัลเล่ต์

praise *(พเรส)* praising, praised

The teacher is praising Peter for the improvement in his school work.

คุณครูชมปีเตอร์ที่ทำการบ้านได้ดีขึ้น

prepare *(พริแพ')* preparing, prepared

Father is preparing the fruit for dinner. He is cutting it.

คุณพ่อกำลังเตรียมผลไม้สำหรับ อาหารมื้อเย็น เขากำลังผ่าผลไม้

present *(พริเสนท')* presenting, presented

Andy is presenting his mother with a bunch of roses.

แอนดีกำลังมอบช่อดอกกุหลาบให้ แม่ของเขา

press *(พเร็ซ)* pressing, pressed

Press this button to start the machine.

กดปุ่มนี้เพื่อติดเครื่อง

pretend *(พริเทนด์´)* pretending, pretended

Willy is pretending to be a ghost.

วิลลีกำลังปลอมตัวเป็นผี

prick *(พริค)* pricking, pricked

A thorn pricked her finger when Helen was cutting the roses.

ขณะที่เฮเลนกำลังตัดดอกกุหลาบ หนามได้แทงนิ้วมือของเธอ

print *(พรินท)* printing, printed

The machine prints posters.

เครื่องจักรพิมพ์แผ่นภาพออกมา

promise *(พรอม' อิซ)* promising, promised

'I promise to look after it well,' said Simon. 'I will feed it and clean it.'

ซิมมอนกล่าวว่า "ผมสัญญาว่าจะดู แลมันอย่างดี จะให้อาหารและทำ ความสะอาดมัน"

protect *(พโระเทคท')* protecting, protected

The shell of the snail protects it from harm.

เปลือกของหอยทากปกป้องตัวมัน จากอันตราย

pull *(พุล)* pulling, pulled

The elephant is pulling the log out of the forest.

ช้างกำลังลากซุงออกมาจากป่า

pull down *(พุล ดาวน)*

The workman is pulling

down the house.

คนทำงานกำลังรื้อบ้านลงมา

pull out *(พุล เอ๊าท)*

Andy's tooth was loose, so the
dentist pulled it out.

ฟันของแอนดีโยก ดังนั้นหมอฟันจึง
ถอนมันออก

pump *(พัมพ)* pumping, pumped

Bobby pumps up his bicycle.

บ๊อบบีสูบลมรถจักรยานของเขา

punish *(พัน′อิฌ)* punishing, punished

Andy was punishing for
being naughty.

แอนดีถูกลงโทษ เพราะความซุกซน

purr *(เพอ)* purring, purred

Our cat purrs when you pat
her.

แมวของเราทำเสียงคราง   เมื่อคุณ

ลูบตัวมัน

push *(พุฌ)* pushing, pushed

Jimmy is pushing the box up the hill.

จิมมีกำลังเข็นกล่องขึ้นเนิน

put *(พุท)* putting, put

Peter is putting his coins into his money box.

ปีเตอร์กำลังหยอดเหรียญใส่กระปุก ออมสิน

put away *(พุท อะเว)*

Helen puts away her toys after playing with them.

เฮเลนเอาของเล่นไปเก็บหลังจากที่ เธอเล่นเสร็จแล้ว

puzzle *(พัส´ สึล)* puzzling, puzzled

The men puzzled over the huge footprint in the snow.

ชายหลายคนพิศวงกับรอยเท้าขนาด
มหึมาบนพื้นหิมะ

Q

quack *(คแว็ค)* quacking, quacked

The ducks quack when the
farmer comes to feed them.
เป็ดร้องก๊าบ ๆ เมื่อชาวนามาให้อา-
หารพวกมัน

quarrel *(ควอ'เร็ล)* quarrelling, quarrelled

Mandy and Helen are quar-
relling over the torn story-
book.
แมนดีกับเฮเลนกำลังทะเลาะกันเรื่อง
หนังสือนิทานที่ฉีกขาด

quarter *(ควอ'เทอะ)* quartering, quartered

Aunt Molly quartered the

cake.

ป้ามอลลีแบ่งเค้กออกเป็นสี่ส่วน

question *(คเวซ´ ชัน)* questioning, questioned

The policeman questioned Jimmy to find out how the accident happened.

เจ้าหน้าที่ตำรวจสอบถามจิมมี เพื่อ จะหาสาเหตุของอุบัติเหตุ

queue up *(คยู อัพ)*

The children are queuing up to return their library books.

เด็กๆ กำลังเข้าแถวเพื่อคืนหนังสือ ให้ห้องสมุด

R

race *(เรซ)* racing, raced

The hare and the tortoise are
racing against each other.
กระต่ายกับเต่ากำลังวิ่งแข่งกัน

rain *(เรน)* raining, rained

It is raining very heavily so
we cannot go outside.
ฝนกำลังตกอย่างหนัก ดังนั้นเราจึง
ออกไปข้างนอกไม่ได้

raise *(เรส)* raising, raised

Peter has raised his hand. He
knows the answer to the
question.
ปีเตอร์ยกมือขึ้น เขารู้คำตอบของ
ปัญหาข้อนี้

rake *(เรค)* raking, raked

Grandfather is raking the leaves into a pile.

คุณปู่กำลังกวาดใบไม้ไปกองรวมกัน

ram *(แร็ม)* ramming, rammed

Uncle Roy's truck rammed a bus.

รถบรรทุกของลุงรอยชนกับรสบัส

reach *(รีช)* reaching, reached

Linda can't reach the book on top of the bookcase.

ลินดาไม่สามารถเอื้อมหยิบหนังสือที่อยู่ชั้นบนสุดของชั้นวางหนังสือได้

read *(รีด)* reading, read

Andy is reading Treasure Island.

แอนดีกำลังอ่านนิยายเรื่องเกาะมหาสมบัติ

receive *(รีซีฟว์)* receiving, received

Andy received many presents on his birthday.

แอนดีได้รับของขวัญมากมายในวันเกิดของเขา

record *(เรค เคิร์ด)* recording, recorded

Kathy recorded the day's events in her diary.

แคธีบันทึกเหตุการณ์ประจำวันในสมุดบันทึกของเธอ

reflect *(รีเฟลคท์)* reflecting, reflected

The moon is reflected in the lake.

ดวงจันทร์สะท้อนเงาในทะเลสาบ

refuse *(รีฟิวซ์)* refusing, refused

The camel refuses to stand up.

อูฐไม่ยอมลุกขึ้น

regret *(รีเกรท′)* regretting, regretted

> Andy regrets that he can't go on the picnic.
>
> แอนดีเสียใจที่เขาไม่สามารถไปปิก-
> นิกได้

relate *(รีเลท′)* relating, related

> Grandfather related the story of his childhood.
>
> คุณปู่ปะติดปะต่อเรื่องราวในสมัย
> เด็กของเขา

release *(รีลีส′)* releasing, released

> Linda is releasing the rabbit from the cage.
>
> ลินดากำลังปล่อยกระต่ายออกจาก
> กรง

remain *(รีเมน′)* remaining, remained

> Willy had four sweets. He had eaten three. One remains.

วิลลีมีลูกอมสี่เม็ด เขากินไปแล้วสาม
เม็ด เหลืออยู่หนึ่งเม็ด

remember *(รีเมม' เบอะ)*

remembering, remembered

Father remembered it was
mother's birthday.

คุณพ่อจำได้ว่าเป็นวันเกิดคุณแม่

remind *(รีไมน์ด')* reminding, reminded

The tall, thin man reminds
Mandy of a giraffe.

ชายรูปร่างผอมสูงคนนั้นทำให้แมนดี
นึกถึงยีราฟ

remove *(รีมูฟว')* removing, removed

Peter is removing his dirty
boots.

ปีเตอร์กำลังย้ายที่รองเท้าบูทที่สก-
ปรกของเขา

renew *(รีนิว´)* renewing, renewed

> Willy had not finished his book, so he took it to the library and renewed it.
>
> วิลลียังอ่านหนังสือไม่จบ ดังนั้นเขาจึงนำมันไปห้องสมุดและต่อเวลาการขอยืมอีก

repair *(รีแพร´)* repairing, repaired

> Our car would not start. The mechanic is repairing it.
>
> รถของเราสตาร์ทไม่ติด ช่างกำลังซ่อมมันอยู่

repeat *(รีพีท´)* repeating, repeated

> The parrot is repeating the same word over and over again.
>
> นกแก้วพูดซ้ำคำเดิมครั้งแล้วครั้งเล่า

replace *(รีเพลส')* replacing, replaced

> The mechanic replaced the spanner after he had used it. He put it back into the tool-box.
>
> ช่างเครื่องเก็บกุญแจเลื่อนหลังจากที่ ใช้เสร็จแล้ว   เขาเอามันเก็บไว้ใน กล่องเครื่องมือ

reply *(รีไพล')* replying, replied

> 'What's your name?' asked the robot.
>
> 'Andy,' I replied.
>
> "คุณชื่ออะไร?" หุ่นยนต์ถาม
>
> "แอนดี" ฉันตอบ

report *(รีพอร์ท')* reporting, reported

> Uncle Roy reported to the police that his truck was stolen.

ลุงรอยแจ้งต่อเจ้าหน้าที่ตำรวจว่ารถ
บรรทุกของเขาถูกขโมยไป

request *(รีเควสท์')* requesting, requested

Hospital visitors are requested to leave by nine o'clock in
the evening.

ผู้ที่มาเยี่ยมผู้ป่วยที่โรงพยาบาลได้รับ
อนุญาตให้อยู่ได้ไม่เกิน 21.00 น.

rescue *(เรส'คิว)* rescuing, rescued

The fireman rescued Jane
from the fire.

พนักงานดับเพลิงช่วยเจนออกจาก
กองไฟ

reserve *(รีเซิรฟ์')* reserving, reserved

This table is reserved for the
Brown family.

โต๊ะนี้ถูกจองไว้ให้ครอบครัวบราวน์

respect *(รีสเพคท์)* respecting, respected

> Jimmy respects old people and gives them his seat on the bus.
>
> จิมมีเคารพผู้สูงอายุและเสียสละที่นั่งบนรถเมล์ให้

rest *(เรสท)* resting, rested

> After hiking all day, Linda is resting her feet.
>
> หลังจากเดินมาตลอดทั้งวัน ลินดากำลังพักเท้าของเธอ

result *(รีซัลท์)* resulting, resulted

> The race resulted in a tie. Bobby and Terry shared the first prize.
>
> ผลของการแข่งขันออกมาเสมอกัน บ็อบบีกับเทอรี่ได้รางวัลที่หนึ่งทั้งคู่

return *(รีเทิร์น´)* returning, returned

> Father returns from work at 5.30 p.m.
>
> คุณพ่อกลับจากทำงานเวลา 17.30น.

reveal *(รีวีล´)* revealing, revealed

> The artist removed the sheet and revealed the statue.
>
> ช่างศิลป์เอาแผ่นกระดาษออกเผยให้เห็นรูปปั้น

reverse *(รีเวิร์ส´)* reversing, reversed

> Mother is reversing the car. Get out of the way!
>
> คุณแม่กำลังกลับรถ   ออกไปให้พ้นทาง!

ride *(ไรด)* riding, rode

> Jimmy rides a horse very well.
>
> จิมมีขี่ม้าเก่งมาก

ring *(ริง)* ringing, ringed

> The bell rings when you press
> the button.
>
> เสียงออดจะดังขึ้น เมื่อคุณกดปุ่ม

ring off *(ริง ออฟ)*

> Kathy is ringing off because
> her mother is calling her.
>
> แคธีกำลังวางหูโทรศัพท์เพราะว่าแม่
> ของเธอกำลังเรียกเธอ

ring up *(ริง อัพ)*

> Kathy is ringing up her best
> friend to have a chat.
>
> แคธีกำลังต่อสายกับเพื่อนสนิทของ
> เธอเพื่อจะคุยกัน

rip *(ริพ)* ripping, ripped

> The naughty dog is ripping
> the curtain to pieces.
>
> สุนัขซุกซนกำลังทิ้งผ้าม่านออกเป็น

ชิ้น ๆ

rise *(ไรซ)* rising, rose

The smoke is rising from the chimney.

ควันกำลังพวยพุ่งออกมาจากปล่อง ไฟ

roam *(โรม)* roaming, roamed

The girls are roaming around the park, looking at the flowers here and there.

พวกเด็กหญิงกำลังเดินเล่นไปรอบ ๆ สวน มองดูดอกไม้ไปเรื่อย ๆ

roar *(รอร′)* roaring, roared

The lion is roaring because he is angry.

สิงโตกำลังคำราม เพราะว่ามันโกรธ

roast *(โรสท)* roasting, roasted

Mother is roasting chestnuts

over the fire.

คุณแม่กำลังปิ้งลูกเกาลัดอยู่เหนือ
เปลวไฟ

rob *(รอบ)* robbing, robbed

The thieves are robbing the
man of his money.

โจรกำลังปล้นเอาเงินของชายคนนั้น

rock *(รอค)* rocking, rocked

Kathy is rocking the baby in
its cradle.

แคธีกำลังไกวเปลให้เด็ก

roll *(โรล)* rolling, rolled

The ball is rolling down the
hill.

ลูกบอลกำลังกลิ้งลงเนินเขา

roll up *(โรล อัพ)*

Father is rolling up the car-
pet. He wants to vacuum

under it.

คุณพ่อกำลังม้วนพรม ท่านต้องการ
จะดูดฝุ่นใต้พรม

roller-skate *(โรล′เลอะ-สเคท)*

roller-skating, roll-skated

Bobby is roller-skating down
the path.

บ็อบบีกำลังแล่นสเก็ตลงมาตามทาง

row *(โร)* rowing, rowed

Jimmy is rowing the boat
across the lake.

จิมมีกำลังพายเรือข้ามทะเลสาบ

rub *(รับ)* rubbing, rubbed

Willy rubs himself dry after
his shower.

วิลลีเช็ดตัวให้แห้งหลังจากอาบน้ำ

rub out *(รับ เอ๊าท)*

Mandy made a mistake but

she rubbed it out.

แมนดีเขียนผิด แต่เธอลบทิ้งแล้ว

ruffle *(รัฟเฟิล)* ruffling, ruffled

Uncle Roy is ruffling Jimmy's hair.

ลุงรอยกำลังทำให้ผมของจิมมียุ่ง

ruin *(รู′ อิน)* ruining, ruined

The painting was left out in the rain and was ruined.

ภาพวาดถูกทิ้งไว้ข้างนอกให้ตากฝน และถูกทำลายไป

rule *(รูล)* ruling, ruled

The King rules his country wisely.

พระราชาทรงปกครองประเทศอย่าง ชาญฉลาด

run *(รัน)* running, run

Rusty can run very fast.

รัสตี้วิ่งได้เร็วมาก

run after *(รัน อาฟเทอะ)*

Bobby ran after the thief, trying to catch him.

บ็อบบีวิ่งไล่ขโมยและพยายามที่จะ
จับเขาให้ได้

run away *(รัน อะเวย์)*

The thief is running away
with the jewels.

ขโมยกำลังวิ่งหนีไปพร้อมกับเพชร
พลอยของมีค่า

run in *(รัน อิน)*

The thief was run in for stealing the jewels.

ผู้ร้ายถูกจับเพราะขโมยเพชรพลอย

run into *(รัน อิน′ทู)*

The car ran into a lamp-post.

รถชนเข้ากับเสาไฟฟ้า

run out of *(รัน เอ๊าท ออฝ)*

> The car ran out of petrol in
> the middle of the road.
> รถน้ำมันหมดกลางถนน

run over *(รัน โอ′เวอะ)*

> The car ran over a watermel-
> on and squashed it.
> รถแล่นทับแตงโมแตกเละหมด

rush *(รัช)* rushing, rushed

> The ambulance is rushing a
> very sick man to hospital.
> รถพยาบาลกำลังเร่งส่งผู้ป่วยหนักไป
> โรงพยาบาล

rust *(รัสท)* rusting, rusted

> Some of the nails have rusted.
> ตะปูบางตัวขึ้นสนิมแล้ว

S

sag *(แซก)* sagging, sagged

The top shelf sags because the books are too heavy.

ชั้นหนังสือชั้นบนสุดทรุดเพราะว่า หนังสือหนักมากไป

sail *(เซล)* sailing, sailed

Father is sailing his yacht around the buoy.

คุณพ่อกำลังแล่นเรือยอชท์ของเขา ไปรอบ ๆ ทุ่นลอยน้ำ

salute *(ซะลูท′)* saluting, saluted

The children are saluting the flag.

เด็ก ๆ กำลังทำความเคารพธงชาติ

save *(เซฟว)* saving, saved

> Terry saves ten cents from his pocket money every day.
>
> เทอรี่ออมเงินสิบเซ็นต์จากเงินค่าขนมของเขาทุกวัน

save up *(เซฟว อัพ)*

> He wants to save up enough money to buy a pair of roller skates.
>
> เขาต้องการเก็บเงินให้พอที่จะซื้อรองเท้าสเก็ตสักคู่หนึ่ง

say *(เซ)* saying, said

> Linda says, 'I'm going for a swim.'
>
> ลินดาพูดว่า "ฉันกำลังจะไปว่ายน้ำ"

scare *(สแคร)* scaring, scared

> Our fierce dog scares off Simon.

สุนัขดุของเราทำให้ซิมมอนตกใจกลัว

scold *(สโคลด)* scolding, scolded

The teacher is scolding Jimmy because he has not done his homework.

คุณครูกำลังดุจิมมีเพราะว่าเขาไม่ได้ ทำการบ้าน

scoop *(สคูพ)* scooping, scooped

Jane scooped a bucketful of sand.

เจนตักทรายมาเต็มถังถังหนึ่ง

scoop out *(สคูพ เอ๊าท)*

Mother is scooping out ice cream for the boys.

คุณแม่กำลังตักไอศกรีมให้เด็ก ๆ

scoop up *(สคูพ อัพ)*

Jimmy scooped up the kitten from the water.

จิมมีช้อนลูกแมวขึ้นจากน้ำ

score *(สคคร์)* scoring, scored

> Bobby scored a goal for his team.

บ็อบบีทำแต้มให้กับทีมของเขา

scrape *(สเครพ)* scraping, scraped

> Jimmy fell down and scraped his knee.

จิมมีล้มลงและเข่าของเขาถลอก

scratch *(สแครช)* scratching, scratched

> The cat is scratching the flag pole to sharpen her claws.

แมวกำลังตะกุยเสาธงเพื่อลับกรงเล็บของมัน

scratch out *(สแครช เอ๊าท)*

> Kathy is scratching out the words so that no one can read them.

แคธีกำลังขีดฆ่าคำเพื่อที่จะได้ไม่มี
ใครอ่านออก

scream *(สครีม)* screaming, screamed

Mandy screamed when a bee
landed on her arm.

แมนดีหวีดร้องเมื่อผึ้งบินมาเกาะที่
แขนของเธอ

screw *(สครู)* screwing, screwed

Uncle Roy is screwing the
shelf to the wall.

ลุงรอยกำลังขันตะปูเกลียวชั้นหนัง
สือกับกำแพง

scrub *(สครับ)* scrubbing, scrubbed

We scrub the floors to get
them clean.

พวกเราขัดพื้นเพื่อทำให้มันสะอาด

seal *(ซีล)* sealing, sealed

Peter put the letter in the

envelope and sealed it.

ปีเตอร์เอาจดหมายใส่ในซองและ
ผนึกมัน

search *(เซิรช′)* searching, searched

Linda is searching every-
where to find the lost crayon.

ลินดากำลังค้นดูทุกที่เพื่อจะหาดิน–
สอเทียนที่หายไป

see *(ซี)* seeing, saw

Willy sees a caterpillar on the
leaf.

วิลลีเห็นบุ้งบนใบไม้

select *(ซีเลคท′)* selecting, selected

The judge selected the best
painting in the show.

ผู้ตัดสินได้เลือกภาพวาดที่ดีที่สุดใน
งานแสดง

sell *(เซล)* selling, sold

Simon helped his father sell oranges.

ซิมมอนช่วยพ่อของเขาขายส้ม

sell out *(เซล เอ๊าท)*

The oranges sold out in an hour. There were none left.

ส้มขายหมดภายในหนึ่งชั่วโมง ไม่เหลือแม้แต่ลูกเดียว

send *(เซนด)* sending, sent

Mother sent Andy to buy some sugar.

คุณแม่ใช้แอนดีไปซื้อน้ำตาล

send back *(เซนด แบค)*

Rusty followed Kathy to school so she sent him back home.

รัสตี้ตามแคธีไปที่โรงเรียน ดังนั้นเธอ

จึงส่งมันกลับบ้าน

send off *(เซนด ออฟ)*

The soccer player was sent off the field for kicking another player.

นักฟุตบอลถูกไล่ออกจากสนาม เพราะไปเตะนักเตะคนอื่น

separate *(เซพ' พะเรท)* separating, separated

Mother is separating the egg yolk from the egg white.

คุณแม่กำลังแยกไข่แดงออกจากไข่ ขาว

serve *(เซิร์ฟว)* serving, served

Kathy is serving drinks to her guests.

แคธีกำลังบริการเครื่องดื่มให้กับแขก ของเธอ

set *(เซท)* setting, set

> Andy is setting the table for dinner.
>
> แอนดีกำลังจัดโต๊ะเพื่อรับประทานอาหารเย็น

set about *(เซท อะเบาท)*

> Andy set about his homework right after dinner.
>
> แอนดีเริ่มทำการบ้านของเขาทันทีหลังจากรับประทานอาหารเย็นเสร็จ

set down *(เซท ดาวน)*

> Willy set down his books on the desk.
>
> วิลลีวางหนังสือของเขาลงบนโต๊ะ

set off *(เซท ออฟ)*

> The boys set off on their hike at daybreak.
>
> เด็ก ๆ เริ่มออกเดินทางตอนเช้าตรู่

sew *(โซ)* sewing, sewed

>   Grandfather sewed the button
>   on my jacket.
>   คุณปู่เย็บกระดุมบนเสื้อแจ็คเก็ตของ
>   ฉัน

shade *(เชด)* shading, shaded

>   Kathy is shading herself from
>   the sun.
>   แคธีกำลังเข้าร่มเพื่อหลบแดด

shake *(เชค)* shaking, shook

>   Andy is shaking the medicine
>   bottle to mix the medicine.
>   แอนดีกำลังเขย่าขวดยาเพื่อผสมยา

shake off *(เชค ออฟ)*

>   A spider landed on Mandy's
>   hand but she shook it off.
>   แมงมุมมาเกาะที่แขนของแมนดี แต่
>   เธอสลัดมันออกไป

shampoo *(แชมพู′)* shampooing, shampooed

Kathy is shampooing her hair.

แคธีกำลังสระผม

shape *(เชพ)* shaping, shaped

The potter is shaping the clay
to make a pot.

ช่างปั้นหม้อกำลังขึ้นรูปดินเหนียว
เพื่อทำหม้อ

share *(แชร′)* sharing, shared

Mandy and Helen are sharing
the sweets.

แมนดีและเฮเลนกำลังแบ่งลูกอม

sharpen *(ชาร์พ′ พืน)* sharpening, sharpened

Father is sharpening the carving knife carefully.

คุณพ่อกำลังลับมีดอย่างระมัดระวัง

shave *(เชฟว)* shaving, shaved

Father shaves every morning.

คุณพ่อโกนหนวดทุกเช้า

shear *(เชียร์)* shearing, sheared

The farmer is shearing a sheep.

ชาวไร่กำลังตัดขนแกะ

shell *(เชล)* shelling, shelled

Linda is shelling the nuts for the fruit cake.

ลินดากำลังปอกถั่วเปลือกแข็งเพื่อทำเค้กผลไม้

shelter *(เชล′เทอะ)* sheltering, sheltered

The sheep sheltered from the rain under the tree.

แกะเข้าหลบฝนใต้ต้นไม้

shift *(ชิฟท)* shifting, shifted

Willy is shifting the armchair closer to the fireplace.

วิลลีกำลังยกเก้าอี้ไปใกล้ๆ กองไฟ

shine *(ไชน)* shining, shined

> Jimmy shines his shoes every morning before school.
>
> จิมมีขัดรองเท้าของเขาทุกเช้าก่อนไปโรงเรียน

shiver *(ชิฟเวอะ)* shivering, shivered

> It is so cold that Simon is shivering.
>
> อากาศหนาวมากจนกระทั่งซิมมอนตัวสั่นสะท้าน

shock *(ชอค)* shocking, shocked

> The news shocked Mandy. She didn't expect such a terrible thing to happen.
>
> ข่าวทำให้แมนดีตกใจ เธอไม่คาดว่าจะเกิดเรื่องเลวร้ายเช่นนั้นขึ้น

shoot *(ชูท)* shooting, shot

> Bobby shoots at the target

twice.

บ๊อบบียิงถูกเป้าสองครั้ง

shop *(ชอพ)* shopping, shopped

Linda is shopping for a pair of sunglasses.

ลินดากำลังหาซื้อแว่นกันแดดสักอัน

shout *(เชาท)* shouting, shouted

Willy is shouting for help. He cannot swim.

วิลลีกำลังตะโกนขอความช่วยเหลือ เขาว่ายน้ำไม่เป็น

shovel *(ชัฟเวิล)* shovelling, shovelled

Father is shovelling snow away from the door.

คุณพ่อกำลังตักหิมะออกไปจาก ประตู

show *(โช)* showing, showed

The salesman is showing

Kathy some shoes.

คนขายกำลังนำรองเท้ามาให้แคธีดู

show off *(โช ออฟ)*

Kathy is showing off her new shoes.

แคธีกำลังอวดรองเท้าใหม่ของเธอ

show up *(โช อัพ)*

Jimmy showed up only after Helen had waited for him for an hour.

แล้วจิมมี่ก็โผล่มาหลังจากที่เฮเลนได้คอยเขาอยู่หนึ่งชั่วโมง

shower *(เชา′เออะ)* showering, showered

You are dirty! Go and shower.

เธอสกปรกจังเลย ไปอาบน้ำเสีย

shrink *(ชริงค)* shrinking, shrank

Willy's sweater shrank in the wash. He cannot wear it anymore.

เสื้อกันหนาวของวิลลีหดหลังจากถูก
ซัก เขาจึงไม่สามารถใส่มันได้อีก

shut *(ชัท)* shutting, shut

Kathy is shutting the window
because the rain is coming in.

แคธีกำลังปิดหน้าต่าง เพราะว่าฝน
ใกล้จะตกแล้ว

shut up *(ชัท อัพ)*

Andy has been talking for an
hour. His brother is getting
tired and says, 'Please shut
up.'

หลังจากที่แอนดีได้พูดมาเป็นชั่วโมง
แล้ว พี่ชายของเขาเริ่มที่จะเบื่อและ
พูดว่า "หยุดพูดเสียที"

sign *(ไซน)* signing, signed

Peter signed his name at the

bottom of the letter.

ปีเตอร์เซ็นชื่อของเขาที่ด้านล่างของ
จดหมาย

sing *(ซิง)* singing, sang

Andy likes to sing in the shower.

แอนดีชอบร้องเพลงขณะอาบน้ำ

sink *(ซิงค์)* sinking, sank

The boat sank in the storm.

เรือจมไปกับพายุ

sit *(ซิท)* sitting, sat

Andy is sitting on the bean bag.

แอนดีกำลังนั่งลงบนถุงถั่ว

sit back *(ซิท แบค)*

Grandfather sits back while Kathy does the work.

คุณปู่นั่งพักขณะที่แคธีทำงาน

sit down *(ซิท ดาวน์)*

> Jimmy sat down and watched
> television.
> จิมมีนั่งลงและดูโทรทัศน์

sit up *(ซิท อัพ)*

> The teacher told Andy to sit
> up and pay attention.
> คุณครูบอกให้แอนดีนั่งตรงๆ และ
> ตั้งใจฟัง

skate *(สเคท)* skating, skated

> The children are skating on a
> frozen pond.
> เด็กๆ กำลังเล่นสเก็ตบนสระที่เป็น
> น้ำแข็ง

ski *(สกี)* skiing, skied

> Jimmy learned to ski during
> his holiday in Switzerland.
> จิมมีหัดเล่นสกีในระหว่างวันหยุด

ของเขาที่สวิตเซอร์แลนด์

skip *(สคิฟ)* skipping, skipped

Linda is skipping rope.

ลินดากำลังกระโดดเชือก

slap *(สแลพ)* slapping, slapped

Jimmy slapped his friend on the back.

จิมมีตบหลังเพื่อนของเขา

sleep *(สลีพ)* sleeping, slept

Babies look sweet when they are sleeping.

ทารกดูน่ารักน่าชังขณะที่พวกเขากำลังหลับ

slice *(สไลซ)* slicing, sliced

Aunt Molly is slicing some bread for lunch.

ป้ามอลลีกำลังหั่นขนมปังสำหรับอาหารเที่ยง

slide *(สไลด์)* sliding, slid

> Bobby is sliding down the hill on a tyre.
>
> บ็อบบีกำลังลื่นไถลลงจากเขาด้วย ล้อยาง

slip *(สลิพ)* slipping, slipped

> The clown slipped on the banana skin.
>
> ตัวตลกลื่นบนเปลือกกล้วย

slip off *(สลิพ ออฟ)*

> Jimmy slipped off his shoes before entering the house.
>
> จิมมีถอดรองเท้าก่อนที่จะเข้าบ้าน

slip under *(สลิพ อันเดอะ)*

> Mandy is slipping a letter under the door.
>
> แมนดีกำลังสอดจดหมายลอดใต้ ประตู

slit *(สลิท)* slitting, slit

Father slit the wood with an axe.

คุณพ่อตัดไม้ด้วยขวาน

slope *(สโลพ)* sloping, sloped

The path is sloping up the hill.

ทางลาดชันขึ้นภูเขา

smash *(สแมช)* smashing, smashed

Willy dropped a glass and it smashed onto the floor.

วิลลีทำแก้วตกแตกกระจายบนพื้น

smell *(สเมล)* smelling, smelled

Smell this and tell me what it is.

ดมนี่ดูสิ แล้วบอกฉันว่ามันคืออะไร

smile *(สไมล)* smiling, smiled

The baby smiled when it saw

its father.

เด็กทารกยิ้มเมื่อเห็นหน้าพ่อ

smoke *(สโมค)* smoking, smoked

Grandfather is smoking a pipe.

คุณปู่กำลังสูบกล้องยาสูบอยู่

smooth *(สมูธ)* smoothing, smoothed

Kathy is smoothing out the wrinkles on the bed.

แคธีกำลังดึงที่นอนให้เรียบไม่ให้มี รอยย่น

snatch *(สแนช)* snatching, snatched

Andy snatched the toy from his sister.

แอนดีฉวยเอาของเล่นจากน้องสาว ของเขา

sneeze *(สนิซ)* sneezing, sneezed

Willy sneezes all the time

because he has a cold.

วิลลีจามตลอดเวลาเนื่องจากเขาเป็น
หวัด

sniff *(สนิฟ)* sniffing, sniffed

The dog sniffed out the rabbit.

สุนัขสูดหากลิ่นกระต่าย

snore *(สนอร์)* snoring, snored

He snores.

เขานอนกรน

snow *(สโน)* snowing, snowed

It snows in winter and you
can make a snowman.

หิมะตกในฤดูหนาว   และคุณก็
สามารถปั้นหุ่นหิมะได้

soak *(โซค)* soaking, soaked

Bobby is soaking his sore feet
in a bucket of hot water.

บ็อบบีกำลังแช่เท้าที่เจ็บในถังน้ำร้อน

sob *(ซอบ)* sobbing, sobbed

Jane is sobbing because her
sandcastle is ruined.

เจนกำลังสะอึกสะอื้นเพราะปราสาท
ทรายของเธอพัง

sound *(เซานด)* sounding, sounded

The alarm clock sounded at
six o'clock.

นาฬิกาปลุกดังขึ้นตอนหกโมง

sow *(โซ)* sowing, sowed

Andy sows the seeds in the
garden.

แอนดีหว่านเมล็ดพืชในสวน

spank *(สแพงค)* spanking, spanked

Father spanked Andy for
tearing the book.

คุณพ่อตีก้นแอนดีเพราะเขาทำหนัง–

สือขาด

speak *(สพีค)* speaking, spoke

Speak softly! Baby is sleeping.

พูดเบา ๆ เด็กกำลังนอนหลับ

speed *(สพีด)* speeding, speeded

Uncle Roy is speeding around
the race track on his motor-
bike. See how fast he goes.

ลุงรอยกำลังเร่งความเร็วในลู่แข่งมอ–
เตอร์ไซค์ ดูสิว่าเขาไปเร็วแค่ไหน

spell *(สเพล)* spelling, spelled

Linda can spell her name.

ลินดาสามารถสะกดชื่อของเธอได้

spend *(สเพนด)* spending, spent

Jimmy has spent all his
money. He has no money left.

จิมมีใช้เงินหมดแล้ว   เขาไม่มีเงิน
เหลือเลย

spill *(สพิล)* spilling, spilled, spilt

> The baby knocked its plate over and the food spilt onto the floor.
>
> เด็กน้อยปัดจานของตัวเองและอา-หารร่วงลงบนพื้น

spit *(สพิท)* spitting, spat

> The food tasted awful so Andy spat it out.
>
> อาหารไม่อร่อย แอนดีเลยคายมันทิ้ง

splash *(สแพลช)* splashing, splashed

> Andy is splashing water on Helen's face.
>
> แอนดีกำลังสาดน้ำใส่หน้าเฮเลน

split up *(สพลิท อัพ)*

> Terry and Andy talked in class so the teacher split them up.

เทอรี่และแอนดีคุยกันในห้องเรียน
คุณครูจึงแยกพวกเขาออกจากกัน

spoil *(สพอยล)* spoiling, spoiled

Willy's parents spoil him. They put the television and video recorder in his room.

พ่อแม่ของวิลลีเอาใจเขาจนเสียคน
พวกเขาเอาโทรทัศน์และเครื่อง
บันทึกวิดีโอไปไว้ในห้องของเขา

spoon *(สพูน)* spooning, spooned

Mother is spooning food into the baby's mouth.

คุณแม่กำลังตักอาหารป้อนลูกน้อย

spot *(สพอท)* spotting, spotted

Simon spotted a bug on another leaf.

ซิมอนเล็งไปที่แมลงบนใบไม้อีก
ใบหนึ่ง

spray *(สเพร)* spraying, sprayed

> Grandfather is spraying water on the plants.
>
> คุณปู่กำลังฉีดน้ำรดต้นไม้

spread *(สเพรด)* spreading, spread

> Father is spreading the cloth on the ground ready for the picnic.
>
> คุณพ่อกำลังปูผ้าบนพื้นพร้อมที่จะพักผ่อน

spring *(สพริง)* springing, sprang

> The jack-in-the-box lid sprang open, making the baby laugh.
>
> ตุ๊กตาดีดฝากล่องเปิดออกมา ทำให้เด็กหัวเราะ

sprinkle *(สพริง' เคิล)* sprinkling, sprinkled

> Kathy is sprinkling water on the flowers.

แคธีกำลังพรมน้ำให้ดอกไม้

squash *(สควอช)* squashing, squashed

Andy's car ran over a ball and squashed it.

รถของแอนดีวิ่งทับลูกบอลแตก

squat *(สควอท)* squatting, squatted

The policeman squats down to talk to the little lost girl.

ตำรวจนั่งยอง ๆ เพื่อที่จะพูดกับเด็กหญิงตัวเล็ก ๆ ซึ่งหลงทาง

squeeze *(สควีซ)* squeezing, squeezed

Willy is squeezing out some toothpaste.

วิลลีกำลังบีบยาสีฟันออกมา

stack *(สแทค)* stacking, stacked

Mandy is stacking her building blocks.

แมนดีกำลังวางอิฐก่อสร้างซ้อนกัน

stamp *(สแทมพ)* stamping, stamped

> Helen is stamping her feet to keep warm.
>
> เฮเลนกำลังย่ำเท้าตัวเองเพื่อทำให้มันอุ่น

stand *(สแทนด)*

> Andy stands on the stool to reach the cookie jar.
>
> แอนดียืนบนตั่งเพื่อที่จะเอื้อมให้ถึงกล่องคุกกี้

stand back *(สแทนด แบค)*

> The policeman told everyone to stand back from the monster.
>
> ตำรวจบอกให้ทุกคนยืนอยู่ข้างหลังเพื่อหลบจากสัตว์ประหลาด

stand for *(สแทนด ฟอ)*

> What colour stands for dan-

ger?

สีอะไรเป็นสัญลักษณ์ของอันตราย

stand up *(สแทนด อัพ)*

Stand up and give your seat to the old gentleman.

ลุกขึ้นและสละที่นั่งของเธอให้แก่สุภาพบุรุษอาวุโส

stare *(สแทร)* staring, stared

Linda is staring at the chick in amazement.

ลินดากำลังมองดูลูกไก่ด้วยความสนเท่ห์

start *(สทาร์ท)* starting, started

Grandmother started knitting a jumper but she hasn't finished it yet.

คุณย่าเริ่มถักเสื้อไหมพรมแล้ว แต่ยังไม่เสร็จ

stay *(สเท)* staying, stayed

> Grandfather has come to stay
> with us for the weekend.
> คุณปู่ได้มาพักกับพวกเราในวันสุด
> สัปดาห์

stay away *(สเท อะเวย์)*

> 'Stay away from the fire.' said
> Aunt Molly. 'You might get
> burnt.'
> "อยู่ให้ห่างจากไฟ หนูอาจจะถูกไฟ
> ลวกได้นะ" น้ามอลลีพูด

stay in *(สเท อิน)*

> Helen had to stay in after
> school to do her homework.
> หลังจากเลิกเรียนแล้ว เฮเลนยังต้อง
> อยู่ต่อเพื่อทำการบ้าน

stay out *(สเท เอ๊าท)*

> The boys stayed out in the

garden all night.

เด็กผู้ชายออกไปอยู่ในสวนทั้งคืน

stay up *(สเท อัพ)*

Andy stayed up till midnight to finish reading the ghost story.

แอนดีอยู่จนถึงเที่ยงคืนเพื่ออ่าน เรื่องผีให้จบ

steal *(สทีล)* stealing, stole

The burglar is stealing the silver.

นักย่องเบากำลังขโมยเอาเครื่องเงิน

steer *(สเทียร์)* steering, steered

You steer a horse with the reins.

คุณรั้งม้าด้วยบังเหียน

step *(สเทพ)* stepping, stepped

Mandy is stepping over the

fallen log.

แมนดีกำลังก้าวข้ามท่อนซุงที่ล้มอยู่
บนพื้น

step in *(สเทพ อิน)*

Terry stepped in a puddle
and got wet feet.

เทอรี่เดินย่ำบนแอ่งน้ำ เท้าเลยเปียก

stick *(สทิค)* sticking, stuck

Kathy is sticking a stamp on
the envelope.

แคธีกำลังติดแสตมป์บนซองจดหมาย

stick out *(สทิค เอ๊าท)*

Andy is sticking out his
tongue at his friend.

แอนดีกำลังแลบลิ้นหลอกเพื่อนของ
เขา

stick together *(สทิค ทูเคธ' เธอะ)*

The pieces of the broken vase

have been stuck together with glue.

ชิ้นส่วนที่แตกของแจกันได้ถูกนำมาทากาวติดกันไว้

stick up *(สทิค อัพ)*

'Stick up your hands!' said the robber.

"ยกมือขึ้น" ผู้ร้ายกล่าว

sting *(สทิง)* stinging, stung

A bee stung Mandy on the finger.

แมนดีถูกผึ้งต่อยนิ้ว

stink *(สทิงค)* stinking, stank

The rotting fish stinks.

ปลาเน่าส่งกลิ่นเหม็น

stir *(สเทอ)* stirring, stirred

Kathy is stirring the soup on the stove.

แครีกำลังคนซุปที่ตั้งอยู่บนเตา

stitch *(สทิช)* stitching, stitched

Grandmother stitched a pretty bow on the collar of the dress.

คุณย่าเย็บโบว์ที่น่ารักติดบนคอเสื้อ

stitch up *(สทิช อัพ)*

My hem came undone, so I stitched it up.

ชายผ้าของฉันยังเย็บไม่เสร็จ ดังนั้น ฉันจึงเย็บมัน

stoop *(สทูพ)* stooping, stooped

Andy stoops down to pick up the pencil.

แอนดีก้มลงหยิบดินสอ

stop *(สทอพ)* stopping, stopped

Our car stopped at the red light.

รถของเราหยุดเมื่อสัญญาณไฟแดง

stop up *(สทอพ อัพ)*

> Bobby stopped up the hole in the wall with cardboard.
>
> บ็อบบีอุดรูที่กำแพงด้วยกระดาษแข็ง

store *(สทอร์)* storing, stored

> The boxes are stored in the attic.
>
> กล่องถูกนำไปเก็บไว้ในห้องใต้หลังคา

stretch *(สเทรช)* stretching, stretched

> Willy gets out of bed and stretches himself.
>
> วิลลีลุกจากเตียงแล้วก็ยืดแขนยืดขา

strike *(สไทรค)* striking, struck

> Boby struck the ball with his hand.
>
> บ็อบบีเอามือตีลูกบอล

string *(สทริง)* stringing, stringed

Linda is stringing the beads
to make a necklace.

ลินดากำลังร้อยลูกปัดเพื่อทำเป็น
สร้อยคอ

study *(สทัด′ดี)* studying, studied

Every night Peter studies for
his exam.

ปีเตอร์อ่านหนังสือทุกคืนเพื่อเตรียม
สอบ

stuff *(สทัฟ)* stuffing, stuffed

Mother is stuffing the pillow
with feathers.

คุณแม่กำลังยัดหมอนด้วยขนนก

subtract *(ซับแทรคท′)* subtracting, subtracted

Can you subtract six from
ten?

คุณเอาหกลบออกจากสิบได้ไหม

succeed *(ซัคซีด′)* succeeding, succeeded

> Peter succeeded in passing his exam.
>
> ปีเตอร์ประสบความสำเร็จในการสอบผ่าน

suck *(ซัค)* sucking, sucked

> Terry is sucking the juice up through a straw.
>
> เทอรี่กำลังดูดน้ำหวานด้วยหลอด

suit *(ซูท)* suiting, suited

> This dress doesn't suit Aunt Molly. It makes her look fat.
>
> ชุดนี้ไม่เหมาะกับคุณน้ามอลลีเลย มันทำให้เธอดูอ้วน

sun *(ซัน)* sunning, sunned

> Willy is sunning himself at the beach.
>
> วิลลีกำลังอาบแดดที่หาด

support *(ซะพอร์ท´)* supporting, supported

> We supported Willy on each
> side and help him off the
> snow.
>
> พวกเราช่วยกันพยุงวิลลีคนละข้าง
> ช่วยให้เขาออกจากหิมะ

surprise *(เซอไพรส´)* surprising, surprised

> Andy surprised Mandy when
> he jumped out from behind
> the snowman.
>
> แอนดีทำให้แมนดีตกใจเมื่อเขากระ–
> โดดออกมาจากข้างหลังของหุ่นหิมะ

surround *(ซะเรานด´)*

surrounding, surrounded

> Sharks surrounded the boat.
> ปลาฉลามว่ายล้อมรอบเรือ

swallow *(สวอล´โล)* swallowing, swallowed

> The snake swallowed a whole

chicken.

งูกลืนไก่เข้าไปทั้งตัว

sweat *(สเวท)* sweating, sweated

The runners are sweating.

บรรดานักวิ่งกำลังเหงื่อท่วม

sweep *(สวีพ)* sweeping, swept

Jimmy is sweeping the leaves from the path.

จิมมีกำลังกวาดใบไม้ออกจากทางเดิน

swell *(สเวล)* swelling, swelled

Mandy's finger swelled up after a bee stung her there.

นิ้วของแอนดีบวม หลังจากที่ถูกผึ้งต่อย

swim *(สวิม)* swimming, swam

Terry is swimming in the sea.

เทอรี่กำลังว่ายน้ำเล่นในทะเล

swing *(สวิง)* swinging, swung

> The monkcy is swinging from one bar to another.
>
> ลิงกำลังโหนจากราวหนึ่งไปอีกราวหนึ่ง

switch *(สวิช)* switching, switched

> The clowns switched their hats, making the people laugh.
>
> ตัวตลกแลกเปลี่ยนหมวกของกันและกัน ทำให้ผู้ชมหัวเราะ

switch off *(สวิช ออฟ)*

> Mother switched off the light before leaving the room.
>
> คุณแม่ปิดไฟก่อนออกจากห้อง

switch on *(สวิช ออน)*

> Jimmy switched on the television.
>
> จิมมีเปิดโทรทัศน์

T

take *(เทค)* taking, took

Willy is taking the cookies from the jar.

วิลลีกำลังหยิบเอาคุกกี้จากโถคุกกี้

take off *(เทค ออฟ)*

Kathy is taking off her coat.

แคธีกำลังถอดเสื้อคลุมออก

take up *(เทค อัพ)*

Mandy wants to take up ballet.

แมนดีเริ่มเรียนเต้นรำ

talk *(ทอล์ค)* talking, talked

The parrot can talk.

นกแก้วสามารถพูดได้

tap *(แทพ)* taping, taped

Linda tapped Andy on his

shoulder to get his attention.

ลินดาตบที่ไหล่แอนดีเพื่อให้เขาสนใจ

taste *(เทสท)* tasting, tasted

Lemons taste sour.

มะนาวมีรสเปรี้ยว

teach *(ทีช)* teaching, taught

Grandmother is teaching
Kathy how to knit.

คุณย่าสอนวิธีถักไหมพรมให้แคธี

tear *(แทร์)* tearing, tore

Jimmy tore his coat on a nail.

ตะปูเกี่ยวเสื้อคลุมของจิมมีขาด

  tear out *(แทร์ เอ๊าท)*

Bobby tore out a photograph
from the newspaper.

บ๊อบบีฉีกรูปภาพจากหนังสือพิมพ์

  tear up *(แทร์ อัพ)*

Linda didn't like her drawing,

so she tore it up.

ลินดาไม่ชอบภาพวาดของเธอ ดัง
นั้นเธอจึงฉีกมันทิ้ง

telephone *(เทล′ ลีโฟน)*

telephoning, telephoned

The house is on fire!
Telephone the fire brigade.

ไฟกำลังไหม้บ้าน โทรแจ้งหน่วยดับ
เพลิงด้วย

tell *(เทล)* telling, told

Simon is telling Kathy about
his trip to Switzerland.

ซิมอนกำลังเล่าให้แคธีฟังเกี่ยวกับ
การเดินทางไปเที่ยวสวิตเซอร์แลนด์
ของเขา

test *(เทสท)* testing, tested

The doctor is testing Bobby's
eyes to see if he needs glasses.

คุณหมอกำลังตรวจดูตาของบ็อบบี
เพื่อจะดูว่าเขาจำเป็นต้องสวมแว่น
หรือไม่

thank *(แธงค)* thanking, thanked

Jane thanked Peter for the
birthday present.

เจนขอบคุณปีเตอร์สำหรับของขวัญ
วันเกิด

think *(ธิงค)* thinking, thought

Terry thought of what he
wanted for his birthday.

เทอรี่คิดถึงสิ่งที่เขาอยากได้สำหรับ
วันเกิด

think up *(ธิงค อัพ)*

Mandy thought up a good
costume for the fancy dress
party.

แมนดีคิดจะหาชุดแต่งกายสวย ๆ ใน

งานเลี้ยงที่แต่งกายแฟนซี

thread *(เธรด)* threading, threaded

Aunt Molly threaded the nee-
dle to do some sewing.

น้ามอลลีสอดด้ายใส่เข็มเพื่อเย็บผ้า

throw *(โธร)* throwing, threw

Jimmy threw the ball to
Rusty.

จิมมีขว้างบอลไปให้รัสตี้

throw away *(โธร' อะเวย')*

The radio was broken so
Andy threw it away.

วิทยุเสีย แอนดีจึงขว้างมันทิ้ง

tick *(ทิค)* ticking, ticked

The teacher ticked all the
sums that were correct.

คุณครูทำเครื่องหมายลงบนคำตอบ
ที่ถูกต้องทุกข้อ

tick off *(ทิค ออฟ)*

> Benny ticked off the things on the list that he has got for the camp.
> เบนนี่ตรวจดูรายการสิ่งของต่าง ๆ ที่เขามีแล้วสำหรับการไปอยู่ค่าย

tickle *(ทิค' เคิล)* tickling, tickled

> Bobby tickled Andy's feet to make him laugh.
> บ๊อบบี้จั๊กจี้เท้าของแอนดีเพื่อทำให้เขาหัวเราะ

tidy *(ไท' ดี)* tidying, tidied

> The desk was a mess so Kathy tidied it up.
> สิ่งของวางบนโต๊ะระเกะระกะ แคธีจึงจัดเก็บให้เรียบร้อย

tie *(ไท)* tying, tied

> Scouts learn to tie different

knots.

ลูกเสือเรียนการผูกเงื่อนต่าง ๆ

tie up *(ไท อัพ)*

We are playing cops and rob-
bers. We are tying up the robber so he can't escape.

พวกเรากำลังเล่นเป็นตำรวจกับผู้ร้าย
พวกเรากำลังจับผู้ร้ายมัดไว้ เขาจึงจะ
หนีไปไหนไม่ได้

tighten *(ไท′ ทัน)* tightening, tightened

Willy tightened the knots to
make sure that the rope will
not slip off the tree.

วิลลีมัดปมให้แน่นเพื่อให้มั่นใจว่า
เชือกจะไม่ลื่นหลุดออกจากต้นไม้

time *(ไทม)* timing, timed

Jimmy is running round the
field. Father is timing him.

จิมมีกำลังวิ่งรอบสนาม โดยมีคุณพ่อ
คอยจับเวลา

tip *(ทิพ)* tipping, tipped

Father tipped the waiter for
being very helpful.

คุณพ่อให้รางวัลแก่บริกรเนื่องจาก
เขาบริการดี

tip over *(ทิพ โอเวอะ)*

The bottle tipped over and
the ketchup spilt on the car-
pet.

ขวดซอสล้มคว่ำ ซอสมะเขือเทศจึง
หกเลอะพรม

tiptoe *(ทิพ′โท)* tiptoeing, tiptoed

The burglar is tiptoeing down
the hall.

ขโมยกำลังย่องลงจากห้องโถง

toast *(โทสท)* toasting, toasted

> Linda is toasting bread for breakfast.
>
> ลินดากำลังปิ้งขนมปังสำหรับมื้อเช้า

toss *(ทอส)* tossing, tossed

> Helen and Willy are tossing the ball to each other.
>
> เฮเลนและวิลลีกำลังโยนลูกบอลให้กัน

touch *(ทัช)* touching, touched

> Bend down and touch your toes.
>
> ก้มลงแล้วแตะนิ้วเท้าของคุณ

touch down *(ทัช ดาวน)*

> Our aeroplane touched down at the airport on time.
>
> เครื่องบินของเราลงแตะพื้นสนามบินตรงเวลา

tour *(ทัวร์)* touring, toured

> Mandy is touring France with a friend.
>
> แมนดีกำลังเที่ยวฝรั่งเศสกับเพื่อน

trace *(เทรส)* tracing, traced

> Andy is tracing a picture of a dinosaur.
>
> แอนดีกำลังลอกลายรูปไดโนเสาร์

train *(เทรน)* training, trained

> The trainer is training the elephant to stand on its back legs.
>
> ครูฝึกกำลังฝึกช้างให้ยืนด้วยสองขาหลัง

trap *(แทรพ)* trapping, trapped

> The fox is trapped by its tail.
>
> หางของสุนัขจิ้งจอกติดกับดัก

travel *(แทรฟเวิล)* travelling, travelled

Kathy travels to school by bus.

แคธีเดินทางไปโรงเรียนด้วยรถบัส

treat *(ทรีท)* treating, treated

Linda treats her pet rabbit very well. She feeds it and cleans its cage every day.

ลินดาดูแลกระต่ายซึ่งเป็นสัตว์เลี้ยง ของเธออย่างดี เธอให้อาหารและทำ ความสะอาดกรงของมันทุกวัน

tremble *(เทรม′ เบิล)* trembling, trembled

Andy trembled when he saw a monster coming towards him.

แอนดีกลัวจนตัวสั่นเมื่อเขาเห็นสัตว์ ประหลาดกำลังตรงมาที่เขา

trick *(ทริค)* tricking, tricked

Andy tricked Linda with a plastic spider.

แอนดีแกล้งลินดาด้วยแมงมุมพลาสติก

trim *(ทริม)* trimming, trimmed

Grandfather is trimming the hedge.

คุณปู่กำลังเล็มรั้วต้นไม้

trip *(ทริพ)* tripping, tripped

Andy tripped over a stone.

แอนดีสะดุดก้อนหินหกล้ม

try *(ไทร)* trying, tried

Benny is trying to lift the weights but he can't.

เบนนี่กำลังพยายามที่จะยกน้ำหนักแต่เขายกไม่ขึ้น

try on *(ไทร ออน)*

> Kathy is trying on a beautiful
> party dress.
>
> แคธีกำลังลองชุดสวยสำหรับงานเลี้ยง

tuck *(ทัค)* tucking, tucked

> Mother is tucking the blanket
> in around the baby.
>
> คุณแม่กำลังห่มผ้าห่มคลุมตัวลูกน้อย

turn *(เทิร์น)* turning, turned

> Mandy is blowing the wind-
> mill. See how it turns!
>
> แมนดีกำลังเป่ากังหัน ..ดูมันหมุนสิ!

turn back *(เทิร์น แบค)*

> The path is blocked so Jimmy
> has to turn back.
>
> ทางถูกปิด จิมมีจึงต้องหันกลับ

turn down *(เทิร์น ดาวน์)*

> Father asked Andy to turn

down the radio because it
was too loud.

คุณพ่อบอกแอนดีให้ลดเสียงวิทยุลง
เพราะว่ามันดังเกินไป

turn off *(เทิร์น ออฟ)*

Turn off the bath water
before of overflows.

ปิดก๊อกอ่างอาบน้ำเสียก่อนที่มันจะ
ล้น

turn on *(เทิร์น ออน)*

Mother turned on the television to watch the news.

คุณแม่เปิดโทรทัศน์เพื่อจะดูข่าว

turn round *(เทิร์น เรานด)*

The ballet dancer is turning
round and round.

นักเต้นบัลเล่ต์กำลังหมุนตัวไปรอบ ๆ

turn up *(เทิร์น อัพ)*

>Jimmy turned up late for the party.
>
>จิมมีมาถึงงานเลี้ยงสาย

twinkle *(ทวิง′ เคิล)* twinkling, twinkled

>The stars twinkle in the clear sky.
>
>หมู่ดาวส่องแสงในท้องฟ้าที่ปลอดโปร่ง

twist *(ทวิสท)* twisting, twisted

>Willy twisted the cap to open the bottle.
>
>วิลลีบิดหมุนฝาขวดเพื่อเปิดขวด

type *(ไทพ)* typing, typed

>The secretary is typing a letter.
>
>เลขานุการกำลังพิมพ์จดหมาย

U

underline *(อัน′ เดอะไลน)*

underlining, underlined

> Kathy is underlining all the important words.
>
> แคธีกำลังขีดเส้นใต้คำที่สำคัญทุกคำ

understand *(อันเดอะสแทนด′)*

understanding, understood

> Bobby doesn't understand why the television won't work.
>
> บ็อบบีไม่เข้าใจว่าทำไมโทรทัศน์จึงดูไม่ได้

undress *(อันเดรส′)* undressing, undressed

> Kathy got undressed ready for her bath.
>
> แคธีถอดเสื้อผ้าพร้อมที่จะอาบน้ำ

unfasten *(อันฟาส′ซึน)*

unfastening, unfastened

> When the car stops you unfasten the safety belt.
>
> เมื่อรถหยุดแล้ว คุณจึงปลดเข็มขัดนิรภัยได้

unload *(อันโลด′)* unloading, unloaded

> The strong men are unloading the piano off the truck.
>
> พวกผู้ชายที่แข็งแรงกำลังช่วยกันขนเปียโนลงจากรถบรรทุก

unlock *(อันลอค′)* unlocking, unlocked

> Father is unlocking the door.
>
> คุณพ่อกำลังไขกุญแจประตู

unpack *(อันแพค′)* unpacking, unpacked

> Mandy unpacks her suitcase after her trip.
>
> แมนดีรื้อของออกจากกระเป๋าหลัง

จากกลับมาจากการเดินทาง

unroll *(อันโรล')* unrolling, unrolled

Andy is unrolling his painting.

แอนดีกำลังคลี่ม้วนภาพเขียนของเขา

untie *(อันไท')* untying, untied

Untie your shoelaces before you take your shoes off.

แก้เชือกผูกรองเท้าของคุณออกก่อนที่คุณจะถอดรองเท้า

unwrap *(อันแรพ')* unwrapping, unwrapped

Linda is unwrapping her Christmas present.

ลินดากำลังแกะห่อของขวัญวันคริสต์มาส

upset *(อัพเซท')* upsetting, upset

The cat upset the bowl of fish.

แมวคว่ำชามอ่างเลี้ยงปลา

urge *(เออจ)* urging, urged

Jimmy urged the dog to jump across the water.

จิมมีกระตุ้นสุนัขให้กระโดดข้ามน้ำ

use *(ยูซ)* using, used

Andy is using a blue crayon to colour the car.

แอนดีกำลังใช้ดินสอสีสีน้ำเงินเพื่อระบายสีภาพรถ

use up *(ยูซ อัพ)*

The milk is using up. We must buy some more.

นมใกล้จะหมดแล้ว เราต้องซื้อเพิ่มอีก

V

vacuum *(แวค' คิวอัม)* vacuuming, vacuumed

Aunt Molly is vacuuming the room.

ป้ามอลลีกำลังดูดฝุ่นในห้อง

vanish *(แวน' นิช)* vanishing, vanished

The magician waved his wand and the rabbit vanished.

นักมายากลโบกคทาของเขาแล้ว กระต่ายก็หายไป

visit *(วิส' ซิท)* visiting, visited

We visited Grandma at the hospital this afternoon.

พวกเราไปเยี่ยมย่าที่โรงพยาบาลใน ตอนบ่ายนี้

W

waddle *(วอด´ เดิล)* waddling, waddled

A duck waddles.

เป็ดเดินเตาะแตะ

wade *(เวด)* wading, waded

Jimmy is wading across the water.

จิมมีกำลังเดินลุยน้ำข้ามไป

wag *(เวจ)* wagging, wagged

The puppy is wagging its tail happily.

ลูกสุนัขกำลังกระดิกหางของมันอย่างมีความสุข

wait *(เวท)* waiting, waited

Bobby is waiting at the bus stop for the bus to arrive.

บ็อบบีกำลังรอรถประจำทางที่ป้าย
รถเมล์

wake *(เวค)* waking, waked

Be quite! Don't wake the
baby.

เงียบ ๆ! อย่าทำให้เด็กตื่น

wake up *(เวค อัพ)*

The baby woke up because
Andy was making a lot of
noise.

เด็กตื่นนอน เพราะว่าแอนดีส่งเสียง
ดังหนวกหูมาก

walk *(วอล์ค)* walking, walked

Grandfather walked in the
park.

คุณปู่เดินเล่นในสวนสาธารณะ

walk off with *(วอล์ค ออฟ วิช)*

Andy walked off with the

first prize in the painting contest.

แอนดีชนะเลิศรางวัลที่หนึ่งอย่างง่าย ดายในการประกวดวาดภาพ

wander *(วอน'เดอะ)* wandering, wandered

Simon and Linda are wandering through the woods. They are lost.

ซิมมอนและลินดากำลังท่องไปในป่า พวกเขาหลงทาง

warm *(วอร์ม)* warming, warmed

We are warming ourselves round the fire.

พวกเรากำลังทำตัวเองให้อบอุ่นด้วย การผิงไฟ

warn *(วอร์น)* warning, warned

The red light warns you when the machine gets too hot.

ไฟแดงเตือนคุณเมื่อเครื่องยนต์ร้อน
เกินไป

wash *(วอช)* washing, washed

Linda washed her hands after
playing with the clay.

ลินดาล้างมือของเธอหลังจากเล่น
ดินเหนียวแล้ว

wash up *(วอช อัพ)*

Kathy washes up the dishes
after dinner.

แคธีล้างจานหลังจากทานอาหารเย็น

waste *(เวสท)* wasting, wasted

Turn off the lights so you
don't waste electricity.

ปิดไฟเสีย จะได้ไม่เปลืองไฟ

watch *(วอช)* watching, watched

Bobby is watching a game of
football on television.

บ็อบบีกำลังชมฟุตบอลทางโทรทัศน์

watch out *(วอช เอ๊าท)*

You must watch out for cars when you across the road.

คุณต้องระวังรถขณะที่ข้ามถนน

watch over *(วอช โอเวอะ)*

The mother hen watches over her chickens to make sure they are safe.

แม่ไก่คอยเฝ้าดูลูกเจี๊ยบเพื่อแน่ใจว่าลูก ๆ ปลอดภัย

water *(วอ'เทอะ)* watering, watered

Mandy waters her plants every day.

แมนดีรดน้ำต้นไม้ของเธอทุกวัน

wave *(เวฟว)* waving, waved

Kathy is waving goodbye to her friend.

แคธีกำลังโบกมือลาเพื่อน

wear *(แวร์)* wearing, worn

Kathy is wearing her mother's shoes.

แคธีกำลังสวมรองเท้าของแม่เธอ

wear out *(แวร์ เอ๊าท)*

Jimmy's shoes have holes in
them. They are worn out.

รองเท้าของจิมมีเป็นรูพรุนเพราะใช้
มานาน

weave *(วีฟว)* weaving, wove

Mandy is weaving a basket.

แมนดีกำลังสานตะกร้า

weep *(วีพ)* weeping, wept

Jane is weeping over her broken doll.

เจนกำลังร้องไห้กับตุ๊กตาที่มันหักไป
ของเธอ

weigh *(เว)* weighing, weighed

> The butcher is weighing the
> meat.
> พ่อค้าเนื้อกำลังชั่งเนื้อ

welcome *(เวล´คัม)* welcoming, welcomed

> Kathy welcomes her aunt
> with flowers.
> แคธีต้อนรับน้าของเธอด้วยดอกไม้

wet *(เวท)* wetting, wetted

> Bobby wet his shoes when he
> stepped into a puddle.
> บ็อบบีทำรองเท้าตัวเองเปียก เมื่อไป
> เหยียบลงในแอ่งน้ำ

wheel *(วีล)* wheeling, wheeled

> The nurse is wheeling Willy
> down the corridor.
> พยาบาลกำลังเข็นวิลลีไปตามทาง
> เดินระหว่างตึก

whip *(วิพ)* whipping, whipped

>Linda is whipping the cream
>for the apple pie.
>ลินดากำลังตีครีมให้เข้ากันเพื่อทำ
>พายแอปเปิ้ล

whisper *(วิส′เพอะ)* whispering, whispered

>Whisper the secret so only I
>can hear you.
>กระซิบบอกความลับมา   ฉันจะได้
>ได้ยินคนเดียวเท่านั้น

whistle *(วิส′เซิล)* whistling, whistled

>Jimmy is whistling for his
>dog.
>จิมมีกำลังเป่านกหวีดเรียกสุนัขของ
>เขา

win *(วิน)* winning, won

>My pet dog won first prize at
>the dog show.

สุนัขสัตว์เลี้ยงของผมได้รางวัลที่หนึ่ง
ในงานแสดงสุนัข

wind *(ไวนด)* winding, winded

The road winds around the
hill.

ถนนคดเคี้ยวรอบเนินเขา

wind up *(ไวนด อัพ)*

Father winds up the grandfather clock once a week.

คุณพ่อไขลานนาฬิกาของคุณปู่สัป–
ดาห์ละครั้ง

wink *(วิงค)* winking, winked

Willy winked at me.

วิลลีขยิบตาใส่ฉัน

wipe *(ไวพ)* wiping, wiped

Andy is wiping his wet hands
on the cloth.

แอนดีกำลังเช็ดมือที่เปียกน้ำด้วยผ้า

เช็ดมือ

wish *(วิช)* wishing, wished

> Andy wished that he had never gone for a ride with Uncle Roy.
>
> แอนดีภาวนาว่าขอให้เขาอย่าต้องไป ขี่รถกับลุงรอยเลย

wonder *(วัน′เดอะ)* wondering, wondered

> Simon can't find his cat. He wonders where she is.
>
> ซิมมอนหาแมวของเขาไม่พบ เขา ประหลาดใจว่ามันไปอยู่ที่ไหน

work *(เวิร์ค)* working, worked

> Mr. Hart works as an engine driver.
>
> คุณฮาร์ททำงานเป็นคนขับรถจักร

work out *(เวิร์ค เอ๊าท)*

> The teacher is working out

the answer to the sum on the blackboard.

คุณครูกำลังเขียนคำตอบผลของการบวกบนกระดานดำ

worry *(เวอ′รี่)* worrying, worried

Andy is worried about his sick grandmother.

แอนดี้รู้สึกกังวลเกี่ยวกับอาการป่วยของปู่

wound *(วูนด)* wounding, wounded

Soldier was wounded in the shoulder.

ทหารได้รับบาดเจ็บที่ไหล่

wrap *(แรพ)* wrapping, wrapped

Mandy is wrapping up the birthday present.

แมนดี้กำลังห่อของขวัญวันเกิด

wriggle *(ริก' เกิล)* wriggling, wriggled

The worms wriggled around in the jar.

หนอนไต่ไปรอบ ๆ โถ

wring *(ริง)* wringing, wrung

Mother is wringing the water out of the cloth.

คุณแม่กำลังบิดน้ำออกจากผ้า

wrinkle *(ริง' เคิล)* wrinkling, wrinkled

When Uncle Tom frowns he wrinkles his forehead.

เมื่อลุงทอมขมวดคิ้ว หน้าผากของ เขาจะย่น

write *(ไรท)* writing, wrote

Linda is writing a letter to her cousin.

ลินดากำลังเขียนจดหมายถึงลูกพี่ ลูกน้องของเธอ

write down *(ไรท เดาวน์)*

> Aunt Molly is writing down the shopping list so she will not forget what to buy.
>
> ป้ามอลลีกำลังเขียนรายการซื้อของ เพื่อเธอจะได้ไม่ลืมสิ่งที่ต้องการจะ ซื้อ

Y

yawn *(ยอน)* yawning, yawned

> When you are tired you yawn.
>
> เมื่อคุณรู้สึกเหนื่อยคุณหาว

yell *(เยล)* yelling, yelled

> That baby is yelling for his mother.
>
> เด็กเล็ก ๆ นั้นกำลังร้องไห้หาแม่

Z

zip *(ซิพ)* zipping, zipped

> Jimmy zipped up his jacket.
>
> จิมมีรูดซิปเสื้อแจ็คเก็ตของเขา

zoom *(ซูม)* zooming, zoomed

> The car zoomed past us.
>
> รถยนต์แล่นผ่านพวกเราไปอย่าง
> รวดเร็วด้วยเสียงกระหึ่ม

INDEX